He Speaks to You

He Speaks to You

Sister Helena Burns, FSP

BOOKS & MEDIA
Boston

Library of Congress Cataloging-in-Publication Data

Burns, Helena Raphael.

  He speaks to you / Helena Raphael Burns.

    p. cm.

  ISBN-13: 978-0-8198-3419-5

  ISBN-10: 0-8198-3419-X

  1. Devotional calendars--Catholic Church. 2. Christian women--Prayers and devotions.
I. Title.

  BX2170.C56B866 2012

  242'.643--dc23

                                        2011046787

Cover design by Rosana Usselmann

Cover photo: istockphoto.com/ © Igor Demchenkov

Published by Pauline Books & Media, 50 Saint Pauls Avenue, Boston, MA 02130-3491

Printed in the U.S.A.

www.pauline.org

Pauline Books & Media is the publishing house of the Daughters of St. Paul, an international
congregation of women religious serving the Church with the communications media.

1 2 3 4 5 6 7 8 9   16 15 14 13 12

To my mother, the "original Helena,"
and to all my nunnies who made this book possible:
Sr. Carmen Christi, who got the ball rolling,
Sr. Donna William, Sr. Margaret Michael, Sr. Mary Martha,
Sr. Maria Grace, Sr. Mary Mark, and Sr. Sean Marie David,
who kept the ball rolling,
and Sr. Mary Lea, who rolled the ball home.
And to the Love of my life
who always speaks to me.

Contents

How to Use This Book

JANUARY—His Love

Self-image, Conscience, Confidence, Sacrificial Love, Mercy

FEBRUARY—His Life

Necessity of Prayer, Surrender, Mysticism

MARCH—His Cross

Sacrifice, Evil, Loneliness, Suffering, Reparation

APRIL—His Will

Discernment, Vocation, State of Life, Goals and Achievement, Freedom

How to Use This Book

The sisters and I have long talked about wanting to find a simple way to share some of what's been passed on to us with young women, to pass on some of what we know and have learned and hopefully have lived: basic principles of the interior life and how to live them in daily life. As religious sisters, we have the incredible blessing and benefit of something called spiritual formation, where the Church basically opens up her treasure trove of wisdom and shares it with us, over the course of the several years of our initial training. We not only get grounded in theology and philosophy, but also in how to apply it all to our lives in order to grow in God's grace and become the women of God He is calling each of us to be. These common treasures are applicable to every state of life.

What better way to share than through short Scriptures, reflections, suggestions, and prayers? Each day begins with Jesus speaking directly to your heart. Words that console, even as they challenge. Each month has a different theme and although the progression flows from January on (beginning with God's Love), feel free to begin anywhere.

The "To do" section is for those who prefer some practical activity (the Marthas!), while the "To journal" section is for those who prefer to contemplate and write (the Marys!). But of course, we're all called to be Martha *and* Mary, so try switching it up often!

We are very grateful to our friends, the sisters from other congregations who contributed to this book.

Many of the books and other media recommended in this book are available at your nearest Pauline Books & Media Center (see addresses at back of book) or www.pauline.org.

Each of you are so beautiful to Him! May you always open your heart like Mary to let the Word Himself love you and become incarnate in you.

Sr. Helena Raphael, FSP

January 1

Do you have any idea how much I love you? I hope you have heard throughout your life, "God loves you." Do you really believe it? If you don't, talk to Me about what makes it hard to believe.

God's word

"For you love all things that exist, and detest none of the things that you have made . . ." (Wisdom 11:24 NRSV).

Words of Wisdom

Ground yourself in God's unconditional love. This is the foundation of your life. A vocation may be difficult to discern and may depend on many different things, but God's love is constant. Even if it takes a whole lifetime to fully realize how much God loves you, what could be more worth pursuing?

To do

Every day when you wake up, let your first words be, "I love you, Lord." Listen to Him answer, "I love *you*!" Sometimes, let Him say it first.

To journal

What is your earliest experience of God's love?

Prayer

Dear Jesus, I believe in Your love for me because You are God who can neither deceive nor be deceived.

January 2

Do you worry over everything—afraid to make a mistake, afraid you might be committing a sin? Do you think your sins are greater than My love? But that would make you greater than Me! That would make sin bigger than Me! (Can you see Me smiling?)

God's word

"We love, because he first loved us" (1 John 4:19).

Words of wisdom

"God is not looking for rigid perfection. We are not machines; we are human beings. Human beings are sinners. We must humbly accept our human condition. Saints are sinners who never gave up trying to be better. Every time you're tempted to doubt God's mercy and forgiveness, say, 'Jesus, I trust in you.' (Sister Susan Miriam Wolf, FSP, www.daughtersofstpaul.org)

To do

Whenever you feel yourself concentrating on your sins in a morbid way, take your mind off yourself and do a good deed for someone else.

To journal

Write a litany of trust: "I trust in Your love, Jesus, because. . . ." Think of ten reasons.

Prayer

Dear Jesus, even if "our hearts condemn us," Your love is greater than our hearts (cf. 1 John 3:20).

January 3

Do you easily excuse yourself with, "It's really not that bad," "You're only young once!" "I'm basically a good person," "I'm not hurting anyone"? If this sounds like you, ask Me for the gift of a more sensitive conscience, as well as repentance, awe, wonder, gratitude, and praise.

God's Word

"Do not be so confident of forgiveness that you add sin to sin" (Sirach 5:5 NRSV).

Words of Wisdom

"Ask yourself when making decisions, 'What will this profit me for eternity?' Life is short, and we will have to account for how we spend our time. Time is precious! It's all we have. Sin is wasted time. Live in continual conversion." (Sister Mary Thecla Paolini, FSP, www.daughtersofstpaul.org)

To do

Make a good confession on some finer points of your attitudes and actions that you know could be better.

To journal

What do you tell yourself that might show that you take God's love for granted?

Prayer

Dear Jesus, I gaze on the crucifix and remember that Your love for me cost You everything. Give me the gift of repentance, wonder, gratitude, and praise.

January 4

There are two extremes of conscience that I find in My people: scrupulous and lax. The first is tempted to the sin of despair, the second to the sin of presumption. In the middle is the healthy conscience—sensitive to both sin and My unfathomable love. Where are you on that spectrum? Wherever you are, move to the center.

God's word

"I have found in David . . . a man after my heart . . ." (Acts 13:22). "With all your might love your Maker . . ." (Sirach 7:30).

Words of Wisdom

Every evening make an examination of conscience. Look back on everything you have to be thankful for, and then look at how you responded to these gifts from God. Ask forgiveness for where you have failed. Doing this every day will make you more aware of how God is working in your life.

To do

The examination of conscience and the sacrament of Reconciliation are wonderful means for spiritual progress. Go to confession regularly, e.g., once a month. Put it on your calendar for the rest of the year.

To journal

Where are you on the conscience spectrum—from scrupulous to lax? Explain your reasoning.

Prayer

Dear Jesus, make me a woman after Your own heart.

January 5

Why do I love you so much? Because I Myself am Love. It is My nature, My essence. So you see, it's all about you and not all about you! I love everyone as if they were the only one, and I love each one the most. Humans are not capable of this kind of love. Put your trust in My infinite love for you.

God's Word

"For God so loved the world that he gave his only Son, that whoever believes in him should not perish but have eternal life" (John 3:16).

Words of Wisdom

"Life is a matter of love. Our vocation is a matter of love. I used to think I had to be holy to approach God. Then I realized I had it backwards! I approach God to become holy!" (Sr. Margaret Michael Gillis, FSP, www.daughtersofstpaul.org)

To Do

Today, begin to see your life as an adventure in love. Take each thing that happens as a way to learn how to give and receive love.

To Journal

Is love the ultimate goal of your life, your *raison d'être*?

Prayer

Dear Jesus, turn my heart more and more to love. Teach me to love unconditionally as You do.

January 6

Life is all about love. There are so many things to distract you and make you think it's really about something else. But it's not. Love is more than just romantic feelings. Love is more than just an act of the will. There is something mysterious about love, because I am Love, and I can never be fully comprehended!

God's Word

"Love never ends . . ." (1 Corinthians 13:8).

Words of Wisdom

Living a life focused on love doesn't mean you have to change your personality. It doesn't matter whether you're a flowery, romantic person or a practical, down-to-earth realist! Everyone needs to receive and give love. Love is the gift of self.

To do

Read all or part of Pope Benedict's encyclical, *God Is Love*.

To journal

What are some mistaken ideas about love that you have seen or heard? It's easy to fall into common ways of thinking. Do you sometimes live according to these mistaken ideas?

Prayer

Dear Jesus, help me keep my life on track by letting myself be loved, and loving through everything.

January 7

Let My love attract you. If you understand how much I love you, you'll be able to interpret everything, all that happens, within the context of My love. You are never outside the bounds of My love, in fact, there is no escape. Even when you are angry I love you.

God's Word

"O LORD, you have enticed me, and I was enticed . . ." (Jeremiah 20:7 NRSV).

Words of Wisdom

No matter what we do, no matter how we feel, God loves us. Have you ever felt angry at God? Anger is often hidden, even from ourselves, but we need to work it out (sometimes with the help of others). We need to get past the anger so we can live from a place of love.

To do

Today, try to be honest with God about your feelings. Let whatever you are feeling surface, whether it is toward Jesus, toward others, or about a situation. Share it all with Jesus.

To journal

Why are you sometimes angry with God? He knows you're angry anyway, and He can deal with it.

Prayer

Dear Jesus, I thank You that Your whole purpose for my life is to draw me into Your heart forever.

January 8

Bad things may have happened in your life. Do you think these things negate My love, or prove that I don't really love you, or that I'm not there for you? Even though bad things aren't part of My plan, suffering is part of life. Sometimes there is even horrific suffering, caused by natural disasters or by sin. I, too, have suffered.

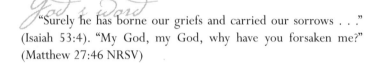

God's Word

"Surely he has borne our griefs and carried our sorrows . . ." (Isaiah 53:4). "My God, my God, why have you forsaken me?" (Matthew 27:46 NRSV)

Words of Wisdom

As you work through your anger and question God, do you try to move on—or do you keep going over things in your mind? Don't let yourself remain stuck in one place.

To do

Listen to the lyrics of Bryan Duncan's "Blessed Are the Tears that Fall."

To journal

Write about the worst thing that has happened to you. Can you see any good that has come of it, or *could* come of it?

Prayer

Dear Jesus, You never promised to shield us from suffering. No one shielded You. Help me to endure. Help me to know and believe that Love wins in the end.

January 9

Everyone can love. I have put that ability into every heart. You can love as much as you want. Love doesn't get used up; it grows when it's given away.

God's word

"He who does not love does not know God; for God is love" (1 John 4:8). ". . . [L]et us not love in word or speech but in deed and in truth" (1 John 3:18).

Words of wisdom

"We have come to know of God's great love for us through prayer, life experiences, the beauty of creation, loving and being loved. Having accepted the love of the Heart of Jesus in our lives, we are called to pour out our love in service to others. Our call is to share the love of the Heart of Jesus through our actions." (Sr. Susan Marie Krupp, ASCJ, www.ascjus.org)

To do

Think of your favorite romantic movie. Does the main character go overboard or *under*board in loving others? What about you, compared to that character?

To journal

What holds you back from loving well?

Prayer

Dear Jesus, love is what makes us human. Help me live my human vocation to love and be loved.

January 10

Are you afraid of My love? Do you think I'm going to ask something too big in return? My love is free. The only thing I ask in return is your love, your heart. Love for love.

"There is no fear in love, but perfect love casts out fear. For fear has to do with punishment, and he who fears is not perfected in love" (1 John 4:18).

Words of Wisdom

God never asks more than we can bear, and He gives the grace to bear whatever He is asking. Even if we fall under the weight of our crosses, He will help us get back up.

To do

This week, notice how you are able to overcome problems with God's help. Notice the little ways that people show generosity toward you. Notice things of beauty that you find delightful. These are all signs of God's love.

To journal

Is there something you fear God might ask of you if you open yourself fully to His love?

Prayer

Dear Jesus, I know it's silly to be afraid of Your love. You are the giver of all good gifts, and Your best gift is love. Take away my fear.

January 11

Are you afraid to receive My love? I am not like some people who lie and betray and grow tired of you and abandon you. You can always trust My love because I am the only one whose love is always faithful.

God's word

"I have loved you with an everlasting love . . ." (Jeremiah 31:3). ". . . [T]he steadfast love of the LORD is from everlasting to everlasting . . ." (Psalm 103:17).

Words of wisdom

Some people are afraid of God because the people in their lives who were supposed to love and care for them fell short. God is the good, kind, caring presence we always want in our lives. Use your imagination. You cannot imagine Him too good. This is the God we worship, love, and serve.

To do

When you're tempted not to "go the extra mile" for someone today, do it anyway. Do it to show yourself what's possible, what you are capable of; to show yourself how God loves.

To journal

Write about a time you felt God's fidelity in your life.

Prayer

Lord Jesus, I cannot always trust those around me. Even with the best of intentions, people fail. But You do not. Thank You for being my rock.

January 12

Are you afraid to love? Are you afraid that you will lose yourself if you love too much? I would never let that happen. I invented you with all your uniqueness! I love you!

God's word

"Before I formed you in the womb I knew you . . ." (Jeremiah 1:5).

Words of wisdom

God doesn't ask everything all at once. Just as Jesus did, we *grow* in "age, wisdom, and grace" (cf. Luke 2:52). That way it doesn't hurt as much!

To do

Take a chance reaching out to a stranger, a cantankerous friend, or a family member today. Did it make you feel more yourself or less yourself?

To journal

Write down qualities you like most about yourself. God likes them, too. How can you grow in these qualities?

Prayer

Dear Jesus, I know I can't lose by following Your way of love. Love *will* change me, but only so that I will be my better self, more like You.

January 13

Love involves sacrifice. Are you afraid that the sacrifices of love will be too much? They will be if you try to bear them alone. I will help you. We will bear the cross together. I will be your Simon of Cyrene.

God's word

"I am the vine, you are the branches. . . . [A]part from me you can do nothing" (John 15:5). "God is faithful, and he will not let you be tempted beyond your strength . . ." (1 Corinthians 10:13).

Words of wisdom

Everyone bears a cross—in every state and stage of life. Ask for courage to change the crosses you can, the serenity to accept those crosses you cannot change, and wisdom to know the difference.

To do

Pray the Stations of the Cross. Pay special attention to the fifth station when Simon of Cyrene was pressed to help carry Jesus's cross. Notice the others along the way who helped Jesus. How did Jesus help them in return?

To journal

Who has been an example of sacrificial love in your life? How can you imitate them?

Prayer

Dear Jesus, no one likes sacrifice, least of all me. But how can I resist following Your footsteps?

January 14

My love makes everything easier—even sacrifice. You don't have to create special sacrifices in your life. As you already know, life brings plenty of sacrifices right to your doorstep. These are the real sacrifices you must learn to bear with love. When you love, they won't feel so much like sacrifices.

God's word

"For my yoke is easy, and my burden is light" (Matthew 11:30). "And his commandments are not burdensome . . ." (1 John 5:3).

Words of wisdom

Sometimes the sacrifices other people make, or those we read about in the life of a saint, seem more heroic than our own. But, the sacrifices of ordinary life can also be heroic. Notice how hard work or boring tasks are much easier when done for someone we love.

To do

Start small: clean up someone else's mess—with a smile! Take on some distasteful chore as your permanent "yoke."

To journal

Write about a time you offered God your sufferings with love. How did it make you feel?

Prayer

Dear Jesus, okay, I get it. Help me to do everything with love. I'm still going to have bad days, but teach me to love through my tears and frustrations.

January 15

Do you want to do something great with your life? The people you can help most are those around you. Give a hand, a kind word, an encouraging smile. Start there as your mission field.

God's Word

". . . [D]o good . . . especially to those who are of the household of faith" (Galatians 6:10).

Words of Wisdom

Sometimes we want to do great things for God. And maybe we will do great things. But the greatest things on earth are people, and the ones we can help the most are right around us. Start there as your mission field. People closest to us can be the most annoying. At times they can find us annoying, too. But God's love is found precisely in this give-and-take.

To do

Name the person in your life that you find hardest to love. Brainstorm a list of ways to help that person and then put your list into practice.

To journal

What are your big dreams of loving? What are your little dreams of loving?

Prayer

Dear Jesus, I would like to love in a great way. Help me start in a small and hidden way, even if no one notices or thinks much of it. You'll notice. That's all that counts.

January 16

You are already very good at loving when you know how to share your-self. What do I mean by that? People don't have time for each other anymore. So show people how important they are to you (and Me). Slow down and give of yourself, your time, your presence.

God's Word

"And Jesus looking upon him loved him . . ." (Mark 10:21).

Words of Wisdom

Find a wise guide that you can talk to about your problems, your faith, your future. If you talk with them regularly, you'll find you're at peace enough to do this for someone else. Fewer people would be depressed if they just had a friend to talk to.

To Do

The best gift you can give someone is a listening ear. "Unplug" yourself and give him or her your full, undivided attention. You can put a time limit on it, but give them that gift. Start today.

To Journal

How do you feel when people don't have time for you?

Prayer

Dear Jesus, help me to find someone wise who will listen to me—even if they can't solve my problems—and help me to be there for others as well.

January 17

Do you know another name for My love? It's mercy. My love is a forgiving love, a love that binds up all your wounds, whatever their kind. Accept My Divine Mercy as it constantly pours forth from My Heart.

God's Word

"Out of his heart shall flow rivers of living water" (John 7:38).

Words of Wisdom

"A terrific piece of advice about prayer comes from the Foundress of the Carmelite Sisters of the Aged and Infirm, Mother M. Angeline Teresa: 'I think the best prayer of all is just to sit quietly and let Jesus pour himself into our souls.'" (Sister Maria Therese Healy, O. Carm., www.carmelitesisters.com)

To do

Think of a river or waterfall you've visited. Remember how it just keeps coming—it never stops. This is how God's grace and mercy is. Imagine yourself in the river or under the waterfall of mercy. Share this image with someone.

To journal

What areas of your life do you need to open to God's mercy?

Prayer

Dear Jesus, I don't want to die of thirst when Your grace and mercy are all around me. Remind me to keep returning constantly to You, my font of life.

January 18

People are called to be merciful to each other. Every time you are merciful, you create a bit of heaven on earth. Don't worry that others won't appreciate or accept your mercy. In My own timing I will make sure that they have the chance to understand, appreciate, and accept mercy. Only through this acceptance can they be saved.

God's Word

"Be merciful, even as your Father is merciful" (Luke 6:36).

Words of Wisdom

It's hard to be merciful because we all want justice. But we aren't in a position to know what is truly just. We don't know another's background, heart, or the graces they have received.

To do

The next time you are wronged, see it as an opportunity for an act of mercy. Acknowledge that you have been wronged, then do something Godlike: forgive. You are extending God's love in the form of mercy and at the same time healing yourself.

To journal

When was someone merciful to you? How was it a great relief?

Prayer

Dear Jesus, being merciful is probably the greatest way I can imitate You. I too am so in need of mercy—from You and others.

January 19

You don't have to earn My love. There is nothing you can do to make Me love you more. When you imitate My love, you are just helping My love to spread in the world; it does not earn you more of My love. Everything I do, I do infinitely. Be like Me: do everything wholeheartedly!

God's word

"Toward the faithful you are faithful . . ." (2 Samuel 22:26 NAB).

Words of wisdom

People can be so cynical—often because they deal with cynical people (and cynicism is very contagious!). It causes them to live halfheartedly, and to discourage those around them. Don't listen to those who say: "You'll see." "You are so naive." "Who do you think you are?" "You'll never be able to. . . ."

To do

God doesn't want us to be foolish, but he doesn't want us to harden our hearts either. Consider what Jesus said, "Be wise as serpents and innocent as doves" (Matthew 10:16). Why do you think He chose these two images?

To journal

Are you wholehearted? What holds you back from living wholeheartedly?

Prayer

Dear Jesus, life can be disappointing, but You never disappoint. You can do anything. You are Master of the impossible!

January 20

When you love, you will have your heart broken and more than once. But this is your task in life: to have your heart broken! I gave you your heart to be used, not for it to dry up! Once your heart is broken, you will feel others' pain, and you will be able to love even more.

God's Word

"The LORD is near to the brokenhearted, and saves the crushed in spirit" (Psalm 34:18).

Words of Wisdom

When we experience heartbreak of any kind—romantic or otherwise—it feels like we won't survive; it's as if we can't go on. But we do. "Earth has no sorrow that heaven cannot heal," St. Thomas More said. Jesus's heart was literally broken on the cross. The blood and water that flowed out gave birth to the Church. Our suffering, too, is fruitful.

To Do

Ask a good friend about an experience of heartbreak. How did he or she cope?

To Journal

When has your heart been broken?

Prayer

Dear Jesus, help me to see my broken heart not as broken, but as broken open. My eyes will now be more open when I love, but I will never stop loving.

January 21

I am not your parents. I am not the police. I am not your boss. I am not a drill sergeant. I am not the voices in your head that condemn and disapprove of you. I am God, your Creator, Redeemer, sanctifier and lover. All day long I am saying, "I love you."

God's word

"[W]henever our hearts condemn us . . . God is greater than our hearts, and he knows everything" (1 John 3:20).

Words of wisdom

"In truth, we desire nothing less than infinite love. Never sacrifice true happiness for pleasure. Always keep that longing for infinite love burning." (Sr. Mary Joseph Heisler, Carmel DCJ, www.carmelitedcj.org)

To do

Become very aware of your inner monologue/dialogue. What are you saying to yourself? What do you believe God is saying to you? Is this really the God of love or is it the voice of discouragement?

To journal

Write about some of the wrong images of God you have had in the past.

Prayer

Dear Jesus, please keep revealing Yourself and Your true nature to me. I want to know the real You who loves me so much. I cannot live without Your love.

January 22

I love you so much, that I desire you to be with Me for all eternity. Why not enjoy the taste of that love now? Take time every day to bask in My love. The more you taste My love, the more you will long for heaven and not be afraid of death.

God's Word

"Therefore, behold, I will allure her, and bring her into the wilderness, and speak tenderly to her" (Hosea 2:14).

Words of Wisdom

As with everything else in life, we grow in our desire for heaven. We are so invested in this life while we are here. Earth is our home, but in a few short years we will no longer be here!

To do

Plan a "desert day" either in your room, out in nature, or at a retreat house. Spend the day in silence, reflection, and prayer. You don't have to be still, but keep silence.

To journal

How strong is your desire to be with God forever? What can you do to increase that desire?

Prayer

Dear Jesus, I'm so busy! Please help me find time to be alone with You and bask in the love that I want to enjoy for all eternity.

January 23

Love is the most powerful force on earth. Some prefer violence, but this is not My way. My way requires that you "do violence" to yourself, that you prefer to sacrifice yourself rather than others. I died so you wouldn't have to die forever. I preferred to be destroyed rather than you.

God's Word

". . . [T]he kingdom of heaven has suffered violence, and the violent take it by force" (Matthew 11:12 NRSV).

Words of Wisdom

It can take effort ("violence") to apply oneself to hidden acts of love, where there is no instant gratification. In an online culture where everyone's a celebrity, am I willing to step out of the limelight and be about the unglamorous works of true love?

To do

Love takes the burden on itself. Today, see if you can relieve the suffering of someone else, even if it causes inconvenience.

To journal

What are some things you value that God probably doesn't value? Might these need to be sacrificed?

Prayer

Dear Jesus, often I want to take the easy way of violence: speaking sharp words, grabbing what I want, threatening, manipulating. Give me patience to do the loving thing, which will require something more of me.

January 24

My word to you, the Bible, has a beautiful, erotic love poem called the Song of Songs. It can be read as if between a wife and husband, or between your soul and Me.

God's word

"... [A]s the bridegroom rejoices over the bride, so shall your God rejoice over you" (Isaiah 62:5).

Words of wisdom

"The oneness to which we are called speaks to us from deep within. We were made for union with the Lord, and as St. Augustine so beautifully put it, 'Our hearts will not rest until we rest in Him.'" (Sister Mary Scholastica Lee, OCD, www.carmelitesistersocd.com)

To do

Read the Song of Songs in the Bible (also called Song of Solomon or the Canticle of Canticles). Memorize your favorite line. Look in a Catholic commentary to help you with its deeper meanings (e.g., *The New Jerome Biblical Commentary*, *The Collegeville Bible Commentary*, *Cantata of Love: A Verse by Verse Reading of the Song of Songs*, by Blaise Arminjon).

To journal

Write your own "Song of Songs" poem about you and God.

Prayer

Jesus, Your love is tender, exquisite, overflowing, overwhelming. Thank You for loving me.

January 25

Desire is a good thing! I have given you all kinds of desires—not to frustrate you, but to let you know what's coming! I will fulfill all of your desires in eternity, so don't bury them. Some desires may be fulfilled in this life, but there is so much more to come!

"Bless the LORD, O my soul, and forget not all his benefits" (Psalm 103:2).

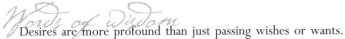

Desires are more profound than just passing wishes or wants. Desire is a great motivator. We need to be aware of what's motivating us. Grow in self-awareness. *Know yourself.*

Take a personality-indicator test like the classic four temperaments or the Myers-Briggs. Did you already know these things about yourself? How does your personality type influence your desires?

Write down your top ten desires in order. What's at the top? Do your priorities need sorting out?

Dear Jesus, I will not kill the flame of desire in my heart, even when my desires seem unattainable in this life. Especially, I will not kill the flame of love, because love is my ultimate desire.

January 26

I have given you everything necessary to live in My love, to be a loving person. Even if you find loving hard, keep trying. Love is not easier or harder for certain personalities. Remember that you don't love on your own strength—you love with My love in you.

"If you keep my commandments, you will abide in my love . . ." (John 15:10). "A new commandment I give to you, that you love one another" (John 13:34).

Words of wisdom

"Where there's no love, put love, and you'll find love," St. John of the Cross said. We can change our environment with just a grain of love. With God's help, even our smallest efforts can have immense results.

To do

Read the First Letter of John. Write down your favorite verse and put it in a place where you'll see it often.

To journal

Write about a difficult situation or relationship in your life and describe how it would change if you put a little more love in it.

Prayer

Dear Jesus, help me not compare myself to others who often seem to have so much more love than I do. Rather let me learn from their example. Increase my love.

January 27

Have you ever tried to love your enemies? It's the hardest thing in the world, but not impossible if you love with My love. Even if you still feel anger and hatred toward your enemy, will yourself to forgive.

God's word

". . . [F]orgive your brother from your heart" (Matthew 18:35).

Words of wisdom

"Forgiveness may be hard, but it brings peace of heart and a sense of joy; lack of forgiveness brings only bitterness. It's been said that carrying a grudge is like drinking poison and then expecting the other person to die!" (Sister Cesira Pierotti, FMA, www.salesiansis terswest.org)

To do

Who/what can't you forgive? Begin by forgiving in your heart. If possible, forgive the person face to face or write a letter. (If you have a painful history that needs healing before you can take the step of forgiving, ask for the help you need to begin the journey.)

To journal

Make a list of your "enemies" and what needs to be forgiven. Make a list of what others need to forgive you for.

Prayer

Our Father who art in heaven . . . forgive us our trespasses as we forgive those who trespass against us.

January 28

Are you trying to drink in all of life? Experience everything you can? You can have everything in Me. I am the source of everything. I created everything, everything is Mine. I want to share everything with you.

God's Word

"Take delight in the LORD, and he will give you the desires of your heart" (Psalm 37:4). "You ask and do not receive, because you ask wrongly, to spend it on your passions" (James 4:3).

Words of Wisdom

Christians are not like Buddhists who try to eliminate all desire. We go to God *through* our desires. He purifies them and will one day fulfill them.

To do

Think of one desire that gets in the way of your desire for the good and for God (for example, to be the center of attention or to get even). Resist that desire today.

To journal

Name five things you feel you must accomplish or experience in life. How will you cope with your desires if they don't all happen?

Prayer

Dear Jesus, I want so much. Life is wide open before me with so many options. Help me to foster desires that are for my good and the good of the world.

January 29

My chosen people of the Old Covenant, the Jewish people, knew that the heart is the center of the person. My Sacred Heart beats with love for you and for the whole world. Do you love Me? Do you love My world?

God's word

"I am the good shepherd. The good shepherd lays down his life for the sheep" (John 10:11).

Words of wisdom

"Know that Christ wants to enter the heart that is open and willing. He will never force Himself into someone's heart. Express your love for Christ by opening your heart to others." (Sister Barbara Moerman, DSMP, www.daughtersofstmaryofprovidence.com)

To do

Pray to the Sacred Heart of Jesus. The image, found on stained-glass windows, in paintings, or as a statue, depicts Jesus pointing to His heart which is aflame with love. Give your heart back to Him.

To journal

How do you show your love for the world that Jesus loves? What gift can you give the world?

Prayer

Dear Jesus, I see in Your heart a love that spared itself nothing for love of me and the whole world. Make my heart expand more and more through every little act of love I do.

January 30

My people can be like porcupines—hard to approach, hard to like. But My people are still the crown of My creation, the apple of My eye.

God's Word

"You spare all things, for they are yours, O Lord, you who love the living" (Wisdom 11:26 NRSV).

Words of wisdom

"People can be unfair and mean, but God's love will never fail you. Remember that God loves you for who you are, created in His image. Do the same: love others for who they are and not for what they can do for you." (Sister Juliana Gapasin, DLJC, www.dljc.org)

To do

Do you relate easily to people or are you shy? People are so important, that no matter our natural inclinations, we need to grow in our ability to communicate well in charity and truth. Find a book or course to improve your people skills.

To journal

What "things" do you love most? How much time and attention do you give them, compared to how much time you give the people in your life?

Prayer

Dear Jesus, not even my good works for others are truly satisfying. Only people themselves are worthy of my deepest affection.

January 31

I am inviting you to be part of something bigger than yourself. I am inviting you to lose yourself in Me, to be part of My plan of love for the world, to make the world My family.

God's Word

"But to all who received him, who believed in his name, he gave power to become children of God" (John 1:12). "So we are ambassadors for Christ . . ." (2 Corinthians 5:20).

Words of Wisdom

Perhaps you don't feel loved. But you are a member of the human race, and every member of the human race is loved by God! If you *do* feel very loved, perhaps those around you filled you with self-esteem. However you feel, be patient, be grateful, and continue to grow in love!

To Do

Where do you see a need for love in the world? Do at least one thing today to help fill that need.

To Journal

Write out your basic worldview in relation to God's word quoted above.

Prayer

Dear Jesus, I'm young and trying to figure out my future. Help me not to be afraid to dare big, to give big, to love big. Show me Your plan for the world and my place in it.

February 1

How can you know Me? You can know facts and you can know persons. I am a Person, one of three Persons in one God. How well can you get to know a person?

God's word

"Be still, and know that I am God" (Psalm 46:10).

Words of wisdom

Prayer is spiritual food. You feed your body every day. How about your spirit? Cultivate your relationship with each Person of the Trinity. Where one is, they all are, so there's no need to fret over giving them equal time. You may address Jesus in prayer, but do you know the Father? The Holy Spirit?

To do

Begin a regimen of daily prayer or examine the regimen you already have. Is it nourishing enough? Do you need to spend more time at prayer every day?

To journal

Write about your favorite types of prayer. Why are they your favorites? How do they help you to know God?

Prayer

Dear Jesus, thank You for being so close to me that I can talk to You whenever I want.

February 2

When you want to know a person, the first thing you do is spend time with him or her. I am with you all the time. Are you with Me?

God's Word

"Set me as a seal upon your heart . . ." (Song of Songs 8:6). ". . . I am with you always, to the close of the age" (Matthew 28:20).

Words of Wisdom

Do you have a personal relationship with God? Definitely! Everyone does because God keeps us in existence. God is already in relationship with us. Are we in relationship with Him? Let's make sure it's a reciprocal relationship, and not one-sided!

To Do

Try to be aware of God's presence. If you have a chance, read the small book, *Practice of the Presence of God,* by Brother Lawrence. Written in the seventeenth century, it is still a relevant read.

To Journal

How can you be more aware of God's abiding presence? What practical steps can you take?

Prayer

Dear Jesus, I'm not alone even when I forget You. Let my heart always keep vigil with You even when my mind can't.

February 3

Communicating with Me is like communicating with people, but also unlike it. That's why there's a special name for it: prayer.

God's word

". . . [Jesus] rejoiced in the Holy Spirit . . ." (Luke 10:21). ". . . [I]t is no longer I who live, but Christ who lives in me . . ." (Galatians 2:20). ". . . [T]he Spirit himself intercedes for us with sighs too deep for words" (Romans 8:26).

Words of wisdom

Prayer is a two-way street. We don't only talk, we listen. When we are faithful to prayer, we begin to understand how God speaks to us. He speaks in a unique way to each of us, because each of us is unique.

To do

Read section four of *The Catechism of the Catholic Church*. It will answer many questions about prayer. (Article 2 is on problems in prayer.)

To journal

Write about a time when you felt God might have been initiating your prayer: the Holy Spirit praying within you. (This might be difficult to determine, because prayer is not only about feelings, and God is closer to us than we are to ourselves!)

Prayer

Dear Jesus, You're in constant communication with me. Help me hone my listening skills.

February 4

You can't have a relationship with someone you don't know, or someone you fear or resent. I want you to know Me as I really am. I want to heal any mistaken images or ideas you have of Me.

God's Word

"Draw near to God and he will draw near to you" (James 4:8). "But for me it is good to be near God . . ." (Psalm 73:28).

Words of Wisdom

"All *real* love is a marriage of souls built on trust. Let us frequently sit 'in the school of Mary' and gaze on the Eucharistic face of her Son. He loves me infinitely! Am I free enough to believe in love—and to love Him in return?" (Sr. Joseph Andrew Bogdanowicz, OP, www.sistersofmary.org)

To Do

Frame your favorite image of Jesus and put it where you'll see it often.

To journal

Write out any negative ideas you have of God, for example, "When something bad happens, God must be punishing me." Then write a corrective to tell yourself each time this negative thought surfaces: "God's love never changes."

Prayer

Dear Jesus, I don't want our relationship to be on-and-off-again. Steady me in Your love.

February 5

I am not like you, always growing and changing. I am constant and immutable. This fact should inspire you to have even more trust and confidence in Me.

God's word

"I am . . . who is and who was and who is to come . . ." (Revelation 1:8). "I am the Alpha and the Omega, the first and the last, the beginning and the end" (Revelation 22:13).

Words of wisdom

Your prayer style can change as you change, just don't stop praying. "In order to pray, one must have the will to pray" (*Catechism of the Catholic Church,* no. 2650).

To do

Get a wall calendar and put a sticker on every day you are constant in prayer. Do this for the whole year. Write brief reasons on the days you weren't so constant. Do you see a pattern? What can you do about it?

To journal

Is consistency easy or difficult for you? What might help you to be consistent in prayer?

Prayer

Glory to the Father, and to the Son, and to the Holy Spirit. As it was in the beginning, is now, and will be forever. Amen.

February 6

There is so little you need to do in our prayer relationship except to keep our appointments and open yourself to receive from Me.

God's Word

". . . [L]et it be to me according to your word" (Luke 1:38). ". . . [U]nless you turn and become like children, you will never enter the kingdom of heaven" (Matthew 18:3). "We . . . take every thought captive to obey Christ . . ." (2 Corinthians 10:5).

Words of Wisdom

Sometimes the hardest thing in a pro-active, do-it-yourself, work-obsessed, rugged-individualist culture is to admit we *can't* go it alone. We act as if the purpose of prayer is to change God's mind, when it's actually to change our own mind and bring it into conformity with God.

To do

In your prayer, carve out time to just receive.

To journal

Do you find it easy or difficult to let people help you, to receive graciously? What gifts are you in need of receiving from God?

Prayer

Dear Jesus, simple as it may sound, everyone who wants to pray needs to recall over and over again the first two steps of a twelve-step program: I am powerless on my own. I need God. So, here I am, Lord: I'm powerless without You! I need You!

February 7

I desire to live with you and in you. You are Mine. You belong to Me. Is this what you want too?

God's word

". . . [W]e will come to him and make our home with him" (John 14:23).

Words of wisdom

There will be difficulties in prayer, as with anything in life that's worth a struggle. Remember that prayer isn't just coming from you, but also from the Holy Spirit in you.

To do

If you don't already wear a blessed sacramental like a scapular, pin, or medal to remind yourself of who it is you belong to, begin today.

To journal

When did you first become aware of your relationship with God? How has it grown deeper? What has helped it grow deeper?

Prayer

Dear Jesus, I want to grow daily in our relationship, and I know there are no limits to how closely we can be united!

February 8

My plan for you involves even more than participation in a human-divine relationship with Me. I want you to share intimately in My divine life—that's what it means to have sanctifying grace.

God's Word

"[B]y which he has granted to us his precious and very great promises, that through these you may . . . become partakers of the divine nature" (2 Peter 1:4).

Words of Wisdom

The word that John uses for "eternal life" in his Gospel connotes that it begins here and now. The sacraments initiate and sustain God's divine life in us.

To Do

Read in a Catholic encyclopedia a definition of "sanctifying grace" and ponder it. Read about the other kinds of grace. Memorize this quick definition: God's Riches At Christ's Expense.

To Journal

How often do you think about the fact that we are called to share in God's divine life? Does this sound strange or even blasphemous to you? (It shouldn't if you understand it as the gift of God's life in us through grace.)

Prayer

Dear Jesus, I thank You for humbly becoming a man. May I accept Your great call to become one with You. Amen.

February 9

Do you understand how much I love you? I want you always close to Me, united with Me forever. I want to marry you, the Church, My bride.

God's Word
"Let us rejoice and exult and give him the glory, for the marriage of the Lamb has come . . ." (Revelation 19:7).

Words of Wisdom
Spiritual writers speak of "nine degrees of prayer." We cannot achieve these on our own, but only be open to them. We don't need to know "where we are." Our part is to love Him in prayer, and try to stay in His grace.

To do
Mystical means "the most real," because a relationship with God is the most real thing in the world. Read about the nine degrees of prayer. (Look for a used copy of *Mystical Union with God* by James Alberione.)

To journal
Every Christian is called to the ninth degree of prayer (called transforming union or mystical marriage). It begins with the sacraments and daily prayer. Take a close look at your daily prayer practices.

Prayer
Dear Jesus, help me remember that I am called to be a mystic. Help me never discount my daily experiences with You, no matter how insignificant they seem.

February 10

I love to give you gifts. One of My best gifts is the gift of prayer. Ask for the gift of prayer—this will set us up for a lifetime of unity.

God's Word

". . . [Jesus] rose and went out to a lonely place, and there he prayed" (Mark 1:35).

Words of Wisdom

"Genuine prayer is simple: be careful not to complicate it. Time spent in conversation with Jesus, aided by Scripture and the Rosary—and when possible before the Blessed Sacrament—will transform your life." (Sr. Mary Emily Knapp, OP, www.nashville dominican.org)

To do

Set up a small shrine in your room, apartment, backyard, or anywhere. It can be as small as a table-top. Arrange it with an icon or statue, candle, flowers—whatever will inspire you to pray. Put a pillow, kneeler, or chair in front of it.

To journal

Even if you don't have much to say, start each prayer session by writing a little something to Jesus about your day.

Prayer

Dear Jesus, if I'm too busy to pray, I'm too busy. Why would I stay away from You, my lifeblood?

February 11

I am the God of consolations. But when you do not feel My consolations, will you still love Me? Will you love Me when you feel nothing at all?

God's Word

"... [H]e fell on his face and prayed" (Matthew 26:39).

Words of Wisdom

"We have to love the God of consolations more than we love the consolations of God." (St. Francis de Sales)

To do

Read more about the dynamics of spiritual consolation and desolation according to the insights of St. Ignatius of Loyola. (See *Discernment of Spirits* by Fr. Timothy Gallagher, OMV.)

To journal

Write about some of the highest and lowest points of your life so far. Do you notice any pattern in your ups and downs? What seems to bring them on? What seems to end them? We can't totally control consolations and desolations, but we can be aware of how they operate. In the high times, remember there will be down times, and in the down times, remember there will be high times.

Prayer

Dear Jesus, You came to bring the abundant life to the mixed bag of our existence. Thank You for life. All of it.

February 12

How does one pray? The Apostles asked Me the same thing, and I gave them the "Our Father." Pray from the heart. If you know how to talk to a friend, you know how to pray.

God's Word

". . . I have called you friends . . ." (John 15:15). ". . . [God] knows the secrets of the heart" (Psalm 44:21). "Search me, O God, and know my heart! Try me and know my thoughts!" (Psalm 139:23)

Words of wisdom

Half of life is showing up, the other half is sticking around. Show up for prayer, and resist cutting back on prayer time.

To do

Try different ways of jump-starting your prayer: play music, read from a spiritual book, close your eyes, burn incense, meditate on an icon, journal, pray a decade of the Rosary, etc. If something that was working before stops being helpful, try something else.

To journal

Journal about some of your recent prayer experiences. How are you being changed by them?

Prayer

Dear Jesus, help me not to believe the lie that prayer is complicated, because that will keep me away.

February 13

There are so many things we can talk about! There are so many ways to pray! So many ways we can communicate! Don't limit yourself. Don't limit us.

God's Word

". . . [I]n everything by prayer and supplication with thanksgiving let your requests be made known to God" (Philippians 4:6).

Words of Wisdom

Perhaps you've heard of the "four ends of prayer": adoration, thanksgiving, petition, and reparation. Here's a way to remember them: A.L.T.A.R.: adoration, (love!), thanksgiving, asking, reparation. The Mass embodies all of these!

To do

Read *Beginning Contemplative Prayer* by Sr. Kathryn Hermes, FSP. Try different forms of Catholic prayer mentioned in the book. Try forms that you've never tried before. Some group forms of prayer (which do not replace individual prayer) are: the Rosary, charismatic prayer, Taize prayer, Divine Mercy prayers, and The Jesus Prayer.

To journal

Journal about ways you could broaden your prayer. Explore the "ends of prayer" that may be missing in your life. Why are they missing? What does your mindfulness or non-mindfulness of each end of prayer say about your relationship with God?

Prayer

Dear Jesus, thank You for continually opening up my world more and more to You!

February 14

When you adore Me, you're doing what you'll be doing in heaven; you are living in perfect accord with the purpose for which you were created. That's why it feels so right!

God's word

"It is good to give thanks to the LORD, to sing praises to your name, O Most High" (Psalm 92:1 NRSV).

Words of wisdom

The greatest adoration is the Mass in which we join with Jesus as He offers Himself to the Father. You can unite all your praise to the prayer of Jesus, even if you are not able to be present daily at the eucharistic celebration.

To do

Sing along with some praise and worship music; memorize a favorite praise and worship song. Read *Power in Praise* by Merlin Carruthers. Learn to praise God in absolutely every situation in your life.

To journal

Write your own psalm of praise to God or write out and memorize your favorite psalm of praise. (Some psalms of praise are 8, 19, 33, 66, 100, 103, 104, 111, 113, 114, 117, 145–150.)

Prayer

Dear Jesus, I thank You because despite all the heavenly praise You receive, You still take delight in the earthly praise we give.

February 15

When you are full of gratitude, you will be at peace and rejoice in everything. You will find jealousy, grasping, overreaching, and dissatisfaction gone from your life.

God's word

"And now, our God, we give thanks to you and praise your glorious name" (1 Chronicles 29:13 NRSV).

Words of wisdom

If you don't think you have anything to be grateful for, you probably won't adore God. If you aren't sure you have anything to be grateful for, start with your existence. It's true that existence is sometimes painful, but the goal is eternal happiness.

To do

Make a list of things you know you should be grateful for. You may not actually be there yet, but keep trying.

To journal

Are you a grateful person? How do you show gratitude to God and others? What does contentment mean to you?

Prayer

Dear Jesus, You are the Lord of my life. I have everything I need.

February 16

Because I am a giving God, you may find yourself saying "thank you" frequently. It is your privilege and your glory to be on the receiving end.

God's Word

"What have you that you did not receive? If then you received it, why do you boast as if it were not a gift?" (1 Corinthians 4:7)

Words of Wisdom

To be grateful, we must first be humble. When we are humble, we aren't easily offended. We are spared much anger and tension. Being humble doesn't mean being a doormat. It means we realize that no one can take away our dignity.

To Do

Let God do His thing. Let God be God. Keep a log of how often you catch yourself trying to run the universe.

To Journal

How quickly do you come to your own defense? Do you make your importance felt? How can you be less combative?

Prayer

Dear Jesus, from now on I'm going to let You fight more of my battles. You do a better job anyway.

February 17

When you ask Me anything, I have three responses: "Yes," "Wait," "I have something better for you." Do you object to any of these answers?

God's Word

"Jesus Christ . . . is always Yes" (2 Corinthians 1:19). ". . . [Y]our Father knows what you need before you ask him" (Matthew 6:8). "[I]f you ask anything in my name, I will do it" (John 14:14). "I waited patiently for the LORD; he inclined to me and heard my cry" (Psalm 40:1).

Words of Wisdom

God is a good Father, not a vending machine or Santa Claus.

To do

"More things are wrought by prayer than this world dreams of," wrote Alfred Lord Tennyson. Keep a prayer list of people and needs you're praying for. Add a column to keep track of how your prayers are answered and also a thank-you column!

To journal

Write a list of your wants. Distinguish which ones are for you and which ones are for others. Distinguish which are material needs and which are spiritual. Of God's three responses, what does He seem to be saying about each one right now?

Prayer

Dear Jesus, You always answer prayers. Give me the faith, hope, and love to always ask.

February 18

I am delighted when you present your petitions and intentions to Me. Don't think I am bothered by your prayers, or wish you would only praise and thank Me! Ask and you shall receive.

God's word

"Until now you have not asked for anything in my name. Ask and you will receive, so that your joy may be complete" (John 16:24 NRSV).

Words of wisdom

There's a great song called "Jesus on the Mainline." It says over and over: "Call Him up and tell Him what you want!" God's best gift is Himself. Ask for the gift of the Holy Spirit.

To do

Make your requests in the name of Jesus. Find a searchable online Bible and see how often in the Acts of the Apostles the disciples prayed in the name of Jesus. This is the Christian way of asking.

To journal

Sometimes "You ask and do not receive, because you ask wrongly, to spend it on your passions" (James 4:3). Do you need to purify your desires and requests?

Prayer

Dear Jesus, You have revealed Your Blessed Name to us. Remind me to use it often and well!

February 19

Will you help Me save the world? Will you offer your unavoidable daily sufferings in union with Me? Because of Me all suffering can now be redemptive!

God's Word

". . . [I]n my flesh I complete what is lacking in Christ's afflictions . . ." (Colossians 1:24).

Words of Wisdom

Jesus made room in His sufferings for our sufferings because He wants to share His work of redemption and His life-giving love with us (cf. John Paul II's *On Human Suffering*, 24). God doesn't need us to save the world, but He has *willed* to need us because He *wants* to share everything with us and make us Godlike.

To Do

Today offer up all your pains and annoyances. Ask Him to use the value these sacrifices have for someone who needs to experience the joy of redemption.

To Journal

What specific sins do you think are most offensive to God? What sins hurt you most? Write down some specific intentions for which to offer up your sufferings.

Prayer

Dear Jesus, reparation is the hardest form of prayer because it involves my own sufferings. But, redemptive suffering is Your way. Give me courage in whatever sufferings come my way.

February 20

I am asking again: Will you help Me save the world? Will you offer some daily sacrifices of your own choosing in union with Me to repair and atone for the sins and injustices of the world?

God's Word

"So, could you not watch with me one hour?" (Matthew 26:40)

Words of Wisdom

Not only our unavoidable sufferings, but also our voluntary sacrifices have great value. However, any voluntary sacrifices we choose must be good for both body and soul. Self-denial is not always giving up something; it can be doing something positive.

To do

When God allows His Mother to appear to us, her message is always the same: prayer, penance, conversion—that is, the Gospel! Read about one or more of her apparitions: Fatima, Lourdes, La Salette, Guadalupe, etc.

To journal

Write down some "permanent" penances you might be able to do, like those things you give up for Lent. Always remember that the Lord wants us to preserve our health. The best fasting and penances are fasting from uncharitableness, sin, and things that hinder virtue.

Prayer

Dear Jesus, help me to live with a penitent heart.

February 21

Do you want to pray surrounded by beauty? Go out into nature, My first book of Revelation. Let the trees, the water, the birds, the weather, the plants, the animals, the land, all speak to you of Me.

God's Word

"The heavens are telling the glory of God; and the firmament proclaims his handiwork" (Psalm 19:1). ". . . [T]he mountains and the hills before you shall break forth into singing, and all the trees of the field shall clap their hands" (Isaiah 55:12).

Words of Wisdom

Since everything was created by God, every bit of creation reveals something about God. The natural world reveals God's power, wisdom, beauty, and love for humanity, for whose sake He made it all.

To Do

Plan some time to go out into nature alone or with friends. Pray and talk about your experiences at the end of the day. Pray Psalm 148.

To Journal

Pope John Paul II—who loved the outdoors—expressed the idea that when we pray with nature, we pray in a perfect way. Journal about times you found God in nature.

Prayer

Dear Jesus, may all my senses revere You in all of Your creation.

February 22

Do you want to hear Me speaking actual words to you? Read My book, My word, My love letter to you.

God's word

"All scripture is inspired by God and profitable for teaching . . ." (2 Timothy 3:16).

Words of wisdom

Ordinarily, in *lectio divina* we reflect and pray over a few paragraphs of Scripture. However, in the daily rush of work or school it isn't always easy to take quality time to meditate. Don't let that stop you. For those times when you are particularly rushed, open Scripture at random. Just a peek at God's word will perk up your spirit like a whiff of fresh coffee, and it will remain to be savored all day.

To do

Look up *lectio divina* online or in a book. (See *Beginning Contemplative Prayer* by Sr. Kathryn Hermes, FSP.) Try it alone or with friends. It's an ancient practice of encountering God in the Scriptures.

To journal

Write about a time when reading or hearing the Scriptures answered a question for you or made you change your behavior.

Prayer

Lord Jesus, thank You for the inexhaustible treasure of Your word. Make me always hungry for more of You.

February 23

Do you believe that you can actually "pray always"? Even though your mind has to be occupied by your duties, just turn your heart to Me at the beginning of each day and let it follow Me like a sunflower follows the sun throughout the day.

God's Word

"And he told them a parable, to the effect that they ought always to pray and not lose heart" (Luke 18:1).

Words of wisdom

"Our Lord had a full schedule during his earthly ministry, but He also made time to talk with God, His Father. You can too. In the morning, ask Jesus to draw you close to Him and to stay close to you during the day." (Sr. Yanory Zuñiga, MC, www.misionerasclarisas. com [Spanish], www.cmswr.org/member_communities/PCMS. htm [English])

To do

Today, try saying brief prayers throughout the day. Set reminders like a phone alarm or a prayer card where you work or study.

To journal

How do you keep in contact with God throughout the day? What can you do that will help set a rhythm and pattern to your daily life of prayer?

Prayer

Dear Jesus, let Your Holy Spirit remind me of You throughout the day.

February 24

Are you frustrated in your prayer? Don't be. Prayer is very, very simple. It's not some task to be uptight over or to execute perfectly. It's just being with Me. Now, is that so hard?

God's word

"My beloved is mine and I am his . . ." (Song of Songs 2:16).

Words of wisdom

Do you find yourself restless at prayer? Do you fall asleep during prayer? Sometimes are you unable to finish your prayers or prayer time? Ask your guardian angel to help you with prayer, to pray with you, and, if necessary, to finish your prayers!

To do

Don't fret over so-called "distractions" in prayer. If some task to be done comes to mind, just write it down and forget about it. Other things that come to mind are often things we *need* to be praying about! Just incorporate everything right into your prayer, like folding chocolate chips into cookie batter.

To journal

Do you complicate your own prayer? How? What are the lies Satan tells you to discourage you in prayer?

Prayer

Dear Jesus, help me not to beat up on myself about prayer. I know You're glad just to see me.

February 25

Do you have the opportunity to visit Me in the Blessed Sacrament? Come as often as you can. I want to pour out My graces on you from the tabernacle.

God's word

"Come to me, all who labour and are heavy laden, and I will give you rest" (Matthew 11:28).

Words of wisdom

Although you may find certain prayer forms more helpful than others, not all prayer forms have equal value in themselves. Jesus is truly present in His Body, Blood, soul, and divinity in the Blessed Sacrament. After the Mass, Eucharistic Adoration is the most transformative type of prayer.

To do

If you can, slate Eucharistic Adoration into your daily, weekly, or monthly schedule. Any church is suitable, but there are some churches and shrines that have special times of prayer when the Blessed Sacrament is exposed in a monstrance, so that the Host can be seen.

To journal

What are some significant inspirations and graces you've received through Eucharistic Adoration?

Prayer

"O Sacrament most holy, O Sacrament divine, all praise and all thanksgiving be every moment Thine."

February 26

You are living in a media culture. This profoundly influences you as a human being. Bring this to Me in prayer.

God's word

"[B]ut test everything; hold fast what is good . . ." (1 Thessalonians 5:21).

Words of wisdom

We need to be aware of the presence of the media in our lives, but this doesn't mean condemning or rejecting it. We have to navigate the world of media by being aware of its influence, recognizing the genuine good found there, and actively participating in media so as to transform our culture from within.

To do

Although we seem to be permanently "wired," try the following. Before you use media, say a quick prayer asking for enlightenment. (See *Media Mindfulness* by Sr. Gretchen Hailer, RSHM and Sr. Rose Pacatte, FSP on media literacy, and *The Church and New Media* by Brandon Vogt.)

To journal

How can you make media work *for* you instead of against you? ". . . [I]n everything God works for good with those who love him . . ." (Romans 8:28). How do various media influence your relationship with God, yourself, your family, and others?

Prayer

Dear Jesus, the media is such a powerful gift. Give me wisdom and discernment to use it well.

February 27

Media is all about communication, love is all about communication, and I am all about communication. If these seem completely unrelated in your life, we should talk about it.

God's word

". . . [A]ll things are yours. . . . and you are Christ's, and Christ is God's" (1 Corinthians 3:21, 23). ". . . [W]hatever is true . . . honourable . . . just . . . pure . . . lovely . . . gracious . . . think about these things" (Philippians 4:8).

Words of wisdom

An ongoing challenge of life is to make sure faith and prayer are not separate compartments, unconnected to our work, relationships, goals, etc. Just as we integrate our faith with every part of our life, we need to make a synthesis of faith and media! This life-long journey requires much prayer. Pay attention to how human dignity is treated in media, and how you treat people with regard to your media use. God can't be hurt through media content and use, but people can be.

To do

Make all media an occasion for prayer. Pray about the news stories you hear; refuse to gossip about celebrities, instead pray for them. Read *Prayer in a Digital Age* by Matt Swaim.

To journal

Write about integrating your media-life with your faith-life.

Prayer

Dear Jesus, I am constantly communicating. May You always be my message.

February 28

You can find Me anywhere, even in the noise and bustle of your life. But I will come to you in a special and richer way in silence.

God's Word

"Be silent before the Lord GOD!" (Zephaniah 1:7) ". . . [I]n quietness and in trust shall be your strength" (Isaiah 30:15).

Words of Wisdom

When God speaks to you in the noise and hecticness, it's usually just a quick inspiration, not "quality time" prayer. As great as media is, we still need times when we're completely "unplugged."

To Do

Plan times of silence, either in your prayer or free time when you can simply lift your mind and heart to God, and be.

To Journal

How do you feel when you are silent? Comfortable? Uncomfortable? Why?

Prayer

Dear Jesus, help me not to fear silence, but face whatever comes up in the silence, with You.

February 29

"I am the Way and the Truth and the Life." Have you ever stopped to penetrate the meaning of these words?

God's word

"Every one who is of the truth hears my voice" (John 18:37). "Follow me" (John 21:19). "I am the resurrection and the life . . ." (John 11:25).

Words of wisdom

The mystery of God is that God is three in one, in a continual exchange of love. Our lives also follow a Trinitarian, three-fold pattern. Jesus, Truth, Way, Life, corresponds to our mind, will, and heart.

To do

The Truth, Way, Life method is the secret to holistic prayer. Divide your prayer time into three parts: *Truth*—What is Jesus saying to me? Do Bible or spiritual reading and reflection; *Way*—How am I following Jesus? Do an examination of conscience and resolutions; *Life*—What am I asking of Jesus for myself and others? Do intercessory prayer such as the Rosary, litanies, and petitions.

To journal

What aspect of your threefold self is strongest? What aspect do you pay most attention to? What do you neglect? Why?

Prayer

Dear Jesus, I am called to be fully alive in You. Help me to integrate all my powers in You.

March 1

Do you have physical, psychological, or spiritual problems? Welcome to the human race. Welcome to My paschal mystery.

God's Word
"But he was wounded for our transgressions, he was bruised for our iniquities . . ." (Isaiah 53:5).

Words of wisdom
Suffering is a part of the fabric of life. Some of the greatest saints suffered from physical, psychological, and spiritual problems. It's precisely how they dealt with them that helped to make them saints. Learn about these saints' varied sufferings: St. Benedict Labre, St. Margaret of Costello, St. Dymphna, St. Joseph of Cupertino.

To do
Offer your past, present, and future sufferings in union with Jesus. Revel (if you can) in their immense, redemptive value.

To journal
The Christian approach to suffering is not masochistic or sadistic. It is realistic. Have you resigned yourself to suffering in a despairing kind of way? Do you fume and rage against suffering? Usually this increases the pathos. Do you need to change your approach to suffering? If so, how?

Prayer
Dear Jesus, Suffering Servant, help me overcome the sufferings I can, and embrace those I cannot in imitation of You, and for love of You and the world.

March 2

What is My paschal mystery? It is the new Passover: My passion, death, and resurrection that have overcome all evil.

God's word

"In the world you have tribulation; but be of good cheer, I have overcome the world" (John 16:33).

Words of wisdom

"From the cross, our Lord invites us to unite our lives—our sufferings and joys—to His. United to His death, we are united also to His resurrection. On the cross, evil is conquered, suffering is transformed, and, ultimately, true glory is revealed." (Sr. Anna Joseph Nelling, OSF)

To do

Look through today's news stories for one that calls attention to the existence of evil in the world and the mystery of suffering. Talk to Jesus about it.

To journal

Write about the ways that those who have truly followed Jesus have changed the world for the better throughout history.

Prayer

Dear Jesus, just as You allow me to suffer with You, help me to bring Your redemption to the world.

March 3

Your pain and suffering will come to an end as will all pain and suffering. Life is very short, so hang in there. Stay with Me.

God's Word

"[H]e will wipe away every tear from their eyes . . . for the former things have passed away" (Revelation 21:4).

Words of Wisdom

"It was sacrificial suffering that redeemed the world and is God's personal gift to me. If I see my suffering in the light of His love, God can and will carve a place within my soul that He can fill with Himself." (Sr. Catherine Marie, OP, www.nashvilledominican.org)

To Do

Make a list of your greatest sufferings and pains. Now tear the page up and throw it away. This is what heaven will do.

To Journal

Write about everything you will enjoy leaving behind and forgetting about in heaven.

Prayer

Dear Jesus, help me remember that "the sufferings of this present time are not worth comparing with the glory that is to be revealed to us" (Romans 8:18). Give me a strong faith and anticipation of heaven so I can do what I have to do and endure what I have to endure here and now.

March 4

Before I came, My people saw suffering as an incomprehensible curse. People thought that if someone suffered, it meant that either they or their parents had sinned.

God's word

"It was not that this man sinned, or his parents, but that the works of God might be made manifest in him" (John 9:3).

Words of wisdom

"Life experience has taught me that Christ is in the midst of our darkness. When we risk entering into the depths of the earth of our own souls and face the shadows and pain that reside within us, we allow the fire of God's love to forge the earth within our souls into precious stones." (Mother Katherine Caldwell, TOR, www.torsisters.org)

To do

Read the Book of Job in the Bible. What was God's answer to Job's protests of innocence during his suffering? Hint: check out some Bible commentaries.

To journal

Write out quotes from the Book of Job that strike you.

Prayer

Dear Jesus, thank You for revealing to us, and especially to me, the true meaning and worth of suffering.

March 5

I make all things work to the good of those who love Me. Even pain and suffering.

God's word

". . . [S]in came into the world through one man and death through sin, and so death spread to all men because all men sinned . . ." (Romans 5:12).

Words of Wisdom

Some question why we have to pay for Adam's sin. We are all spiritually connected (the Mystical Body of Christ), not just physically descended from our first parents. We have all committed personal sins. We have to humbly accept our human condition, which is also now our glory, because Jesus has raised our human nature to a higher status then we had in the beginning.

To do

When we suffer we are given a new dignity in imitation of Jesus. Share this hope-filled message with a fellow-sufferer.

To journal

Once when her cart overturned in the mud, St. Teresa of Avila told God, "No wonder you have so few friends. Look at how you treat the friends you do have!" What is your reaction to this thought?

Prayer

Dear Jesus, thank You for giving me a share in Your sufferings. "If we suffer with You, we will reign with You."

March 6

Taking up your cross is a requirement for being My disciple. But do not be afraid, "For my yoke is easy, and my burden is light" (Matthew 11:30).

God's word

"[H]e who does not take his cross and follow me is not worthy of me" (Matthew 10:38). "If any man would come after me, let him deny himself and take up his cross daily and follow me" (Luke 9:23).

Words of wisdom

In Jesus's time, oxen had custom-made yokes that fit them perfectly. Jesus may have meant that our crosses are "just right" for each of us. If two oxen were plowing side-by-side, the burden would be easier. Jesus may have also meant that our burden would be light because He would be right by our side.

To do

Give a name to your yoke, your burden, your cross. It is the cross of _____. What is "just right" about this cross for you?

To journal

Carrying a cross? And you still want to be a Christian? Describe what carrying your cross has meant in your life.

Prayer

Dear Jesus, I trust that for every burden You will give me the strength to carry it.

March 7

I made you unique. I have given you unique gifts. But along with your strengths, you also have weaknesses.

God's Word

"Though if I wish to boast, I shall not be a fool, for I shall be speaking the truth. And to keep me from being too elated by the abundance of revelations, a thorn was given me in the flesh, a messenger of Satan, to harass me . . ." (2 Corinthians 12:6–7).

Words of Wisdom

"At times you might not feel strong enough to overcome certain temptations, sins or personality defects. Trust that God's grace will sustain you through anything and everything, and truly believe that not even your worst fault can keep God from loving you." (Sr. Lorena Sandoval, MGSps, www.misionerasguadalupanas.com)

To do

Research the seven capital sins. Which one is *your* cross, your predominant defect? Are you working to overcome it? What further steps can you take to overcome it?

To journal

Write about how you experience the seven capital sins tugging at you and their degree of strength. (Some will not even be that big of a problem for you.) Write about each one's corresponding virtue and how you practice those virtues.

Prayer

Dear Jesus, thank You that with every temptation, You give us a way out.

March 8

My suffering and death were horrific, but My love for you is what made Me do it. No other reason.

God's word

"[T]he Son of God . . . loved me and gave himself for me" (Galatians 2:20).

Words of wisdom

"We can't have the resurrection without the cross. The cross is our life and salvation! To live we must die and in dying we rise! When our suffering is united with Jesus out of love, it becomes a great dynamo of grace for souls." (Sr. Melissa Moxley, MS, www.marian-sisters.org)

To do

Watch *The Passion of the Christ*. See every suffering as an act of love just for you. Jesus would have died for you if you were the only one. What acts of love can you do for others?

To journal

When things were at their worst, St. Francis of Assisi would call it "perfect joy." Write about a time you experienced "perfect joy." Did you see it as joy then? Now?

Prayer

Dear Jesus, I'm beginning to see that life is all about sacrificial love. Help me not to shrink from sacrificial love.

March 9

I was not smiling on the cross. You will often not be able to smile in your sufferings. That's okay. Sufferings can be all-consuming. At these times, you are an icon of Me.

God's Word

"I have been crucified with Christ . . ." (Galatians 2:20). ". . . I bear on my body the marks of Jesus" (Galatians 6:17).

Words of Wisdom

Sometimes Christians think they are bad witnesses for Christ if they aren't smiling all the time. But the world knows a fake smile when it sees one. The world will appreciate your honesty. Everyone knows what suffering is like.

To do

Read *On the Christian Meaning of Human Suffering* by John Paul II. The next time you feel the need to complain about some suffering, add words of hope that will identify you as a Christian!

To journal

Suffering is hard work. As her letters reveal, at times even Mother Teresa found it difficult to smile at Jesus. When is it difficult for you to smile at Jesus?

Prayer

Dear Jesus, too often I'm only about my own happiness. Help me to look to the needs of others as my own. I know happiness will follow.

March 10

You will have some very dark times in your life. Do not be afraid—this is ordinary. And though part of the darkness may be feeling that I'm not there, I am.

God's Word

". . . [M]y only friend is darkness" (Psalm 88:19 NAB).

Words of Wisdom

"Find a trusted spiritual guide—if you don't already have one—to help you explore the true cause of the darkness. Whatever its cause, however, know that it represents an opportunity to love the Lord for *Himself,* and not for His consolations or even His light." (Sr. Mary Richard Morris, LSP, www.littlesistersofthepoor.org)

To Do

Read *Dark Night of the Soul* by Dr. Gerald May. He explains St. John of the Cross's *Dark Night of the Soul*. Check out the letters of Mother Teresa that reveal her very long dark night in the book *Come Be My Light*. Pray all of Psalm 88.

To Journal

Have you passed through any dark nights already? What were they like? Did you understand what was happening? Where did you feel God was? What happened afterward?

Prayer

Dear Jesus, You were like us in everything but sin. Remind me that there's nothing I go through that You haven't already.

March 11

Don't discredit any of your sufferings. They are all precious in My eyes and all valuable in My plan of redemption for the whole world.

God's Word

". . . [God] desires all men to be saved . . ." (1 Timothy 2:4).

Words of Wisdom

"We can lose hope in God. God is always with us and will never leave us. There may be times in our lives when we think that God is not with us, and yet He is with us each and every day. God loves each of us individually and will never go back on His promises." (Sr. Darlene Johnson, DSMP, www.daughtersofstmaryofprovidence. com)

To do

Sometimes it's the little things that get us most disturbed. What are your littlest crosses? Name them and offer them to God.

To journal

Just as everyone is called to the heights of mystical prayer, so everyone is called to enter into the paschal mystery which is God's own M.O.! Write about a time you observed this paschal process working in your life: suffering, death, resurrection.

Prayer

Dear Jesus, life really is about the little things. And You have promised that if I am faithful in the little things, I will be faithful in greater things.

March 12

What do you think of the evil you see all around you and even sometimes within you? I did not create evil. Evil has no "being." Evil is a privation of the good.

God's Word

". . . [O]vercome evil with good" (Romans 12:21).

Words of Wisdom

"What a consolation to know that in Jesus Christ we are free from evil. He is the supreme good! Keep your eyes on Jesus and He will be the way to overcome all evil! 'I am the way, and the truth, and the life' (John 14:6). One way to overcome evil is to 'kill them with kindness,' or 'speak the truth in love.'" (Sr. Maria Catherine Iannotti, PVMI, www.parishvisitors.org)

To do

What would you say to someone who claims there is no God because of all the evil in the world? Formulate a response you can actually use.

To journal

In your opinion what are the worst manifestations of evil? Does evil shake your faith? Why or why not?

Prayer

Dear Jesus, evil in the world is a stumbling block for those who do not know You. But I know You, and to know You is eternal life (cf. John 17:3).

March 13

Satan has "being" because he is a person: a fallen angel with his fallen angel followers. "Being" is a good, so Satan, in spite of himself, is not completely evil.

God's Word

". . . [T]he devil has come down to you in great wrath, because he knows that his time is short!" (Revelation 12:12)

Words of Wisdom

Satan's hatred is two-fold: he doesn't want anyone to love the God he hates, and he doesn't want anyone to go to the heaven he lost. If we don't want to be with God, we don't have to be—and we won't be. We have free will to go where we want.

To Do

Look up evil and Satan in the *Catechism of the Catholic Church*. What did you learn that you didn't know before? For further reading check out *An Exorcist Tells His Story* by Gabriel Amorth, SSP.

To Journal

It isn't necessary to worship Satan to follow him. The Satanic Bible is summed up in the phrase: "Do what you will." How do you try to determine God's will in your life?

Prayer

"O St. Michael the Archangel, defend us in battle. Be our protection against the wickedness and snares of the devil."

March 14

The only power Satan has over you is the power you give him. Adam and Eve began giving him that power in the Garden of Eden.

God's Word

"The reason the Son of God appeared was to destroy the works of the devil" (1 John 3:8). ". . . Satan, the deceiver of the whole world . . ." (Revelation 12:9).

Words of Wisdom

God and Satan are in no way equals. One is the Creator and one a creature. However, Satan is stronger than humans. As an angel, he is a superior being in every way. But God limits Satan, and limits evil in the world—otherwise it would overtake us.

To Do

By living a sacramental life, embracing the cross, and practicing forgiveness, we have nothing to fear from evil. Pick one of these three to work on this month.

To Journal

What are some ways that God limits evil?

Prayer

Dear Jesus, I thank You for already defeating Satan at the cross.

March 15

Forgiveness is the greatest power on earth. Forgiveness is love of one's enemies. From the cross I forgave not only the sins of the whole world past, present, and future, but also the very sin that put Me there.

God's Word

"Father, forgive them; for they know not what they do" (Luke 23:34).

Words of Wisdom

"When we aren't free, we hold back our own development and spirit, and that of the Church. He enters our wounds with bloody hands to heal them. He is with you. Invite Him in fully." (Sr. Mary Michael Keaschall, CK, www.cksisters.org)

To Do

Forgiveness is healing: sometimes for the offender, always for the offended. Who do you need to forgive? Think and pray about approaching that person and offering your forgiveness if it seems appropriate.

To Journal

Write down the names of those you still need to forgive. Bring this list to prayer. Truly desire and pray for their conversion and their good.

Prayer

Dear Jesus, I have been badly hurt by people to whom I have done nothing wrong. You were the most innocent, and look what was done to You. Give me Your strength to forgive.

March 16

My love and forgiveness were not intended only for individuals. I intend for the whole world to be My children, My family, My bride.

God's word

"For in him all the fullness of God was pleased to dwell . . . to reconcile to himself all things . . . making peace by the blood of his cross" (Colossians 1:19–20).

Words of wisdom

Nonviolent action is the cross in action. Jesus showed us that we can eradicate evil by taking suffering on ourselves, giving our lives for others. Nonviolent action works! Gandhi (India), Martin Luther King, Jr. (U.S.A.), Truth and Reconciliation Process (South Africa), People Power Revolution (Philippines), political power-sharing (Northern Ireland), penal system (Samoa), etc., exemplify this.

To do

Learn more about nonviolent action movements. Films such as *Gandhi, Eyes on the Prize, Evil and the Justice of God, The Untold Story: The Miracle of EDSA* are great resources.

To journal

How you can practice these six principles of nonviolence: courage, friendship and understanding, defeat of injustice, suffering that educates and transforms, love over hatred, awareness that God is on the side of justice?

Prayer

Dear Jesus, love, forgiveness, and peace are possible on a global scale. Help me be part of the solution, not the problem.

March 17

Everyone suffers. Some people suffer more than others. They resemble Me more than they realize. Will you see Me in them?

God's Word

". . . [A]s you did it to one of the least of these my brethren, you did it to me" (Matthew 25:40).

Words of Wisdom

Some souls seem to be chosen as "victim souls." They have suffering upon suffering, as has been the case for the Jews, God's Chosen People. Jesus reprimanded Peter for not wanting Him to go to Calvary: "Get behind me, Satan!" (Matthew 16:23). Think of suffering as a school.

To do

Visit or talk with someone who has experienced great suffering, physical or otherwise. Ask them what the cross means to them.

To journal

Who do you know that has had great sufferings in his or her life? How does that person deal with it? Are you one of these persons? How do you deal with it?

Prayer

Dear Jesus, I think it's time I laid to rest my notion of fighting with Your cross. Let my first reaction be to see You rather than flee from You the next time I come upon a cross.

March 18

My cross is offensive. My cross is ugly. My cross is brutal, but it is Good News. Do you believe that?

God's Word

"... [P]ower is made perfect in weakness ... for whenever I am weak, then I am strong" (2 Corinthians 12:9–10).

Words of Wisdom

God's ways are not like our ways. The Bible tells us that often "what is prized by human beings is an abomination in the sight of God" (Luke 16:15 NRSV). The more we reason the way God reasons, the more peace we'll have.

To Do

Are there areas of my life I don't let God into? What are they, and why don't I let God in? Do I think I am strong enough to handle them on my own? Make a pact with the Lord to handle these areas *together*.

To Journal

The saints were willing to undergo any tribulations for the good of their souls or for the good of others. We all shrink from sufferings, but with God's grace, we can face and endure anything. What are my greatest fears?

Prayer

We adore You, O Christ, and we bless You, because by Your holy cross You have redeemed the world.

March 19

Suffering is unavoidable. You don't want to run from My cross. If you run from My cross, you may find yourself staring at a pitchfork! I only permit you to suffer here. Satan wants you to suffer hereafter.

God's Word

". . . [W]here can I flee from your presence?" (Psalm 139:7 NRSV)

Words of Wisdom

The first step to facing unavoidable suffering is suffering with acceptance. The second step is suffering with love. Eventually, love takes over. The saints were almost indifferent as to whether or not they were suffering. They were willing to suffer as long as necessary—out of love. And we're all called to be saints, right?

To do

Love always seems to involve some suffering, something very evident in love songs! Listen to some love songs that could be applied to Jesus and you.

To journal

What distinctions do you see when considering your random sufferings, sufferings you bring on yourself because of bad choices, and sufferings you bring on yourself because of the good you've chosen?

Prayer

Dear Jesus, they say that no good deed goes unpunished, but in the end, the distinctions in my sufferings aren't important, only the love.

March 20

The world is watching to see how you, My followers, accept crosses and tragedies, big and small. Are you as sad, angry, impatient, and demanding as those unacquainted with My cross?

God's word

"[A]nd if any one forces you to go one mile, go with him two miles" (Matthew 5:41).

Words of Wisdom

It's good to seek healing for our wounds, but only heaven will completely heal all wounds. Sometimes we must learn to live with certain hurts or at least scars. In *A Step Further,* Joni Eareckson Tada, a quadriplegic, gives practical tips about suffering with grace, style, and a sense of humor. The movie *Soul Surfer* shows thirteen-year-old surfer Bethany Hamilton's trauma and triumph after a shark attack.

To do

The next time you're cut off in traffic or have a bad customer service experience, surprise everyone, including yourself, by responding graciously.

To journal

How we carry crosses becomes a great tool of evangelization. How have people witnessed to you by carrying their crosses? How have you witnessed to others by carrying your cross?

Prayer

Dear Jesus, You had concern for others even on Your sorrowful *Via Dolorosa.* Teach me this same self-forgetfulness.

March 21

Although you will never fully comprehend Me, in time or eternity, I have revealed to you extraordinary mysteries: the Trinity, the cross, love. I have nothing more I can give you.

God's Word

"To you it has been given to know the secrets of the kingdom of God . . ." (Luke 8:10).

Words of Wisdom

The Brothers Karamazov probes the causes of children's sufferings. Even if a beautiful heaven awaits them, children shouldn't have to suffer here and now. It's wise to think about sufferings *before* they come, and find ways to answer for yourself and others the perennial "problem of evil."

To do

Think about how the Trinity, the cross, and love are also the answer to the above problem. Read C. S. Lewis's small book *The Problem of Pain*.

To journal

God asks, "Do you trust Me?" We don't see things played out fully in this life. Our trust must stretch beyond this life. Reflect on your own distrust or trust of God.

Prayer

Dear Jesus, You created a universe in which, because of human freedom, sin and evil are possible. Freedom is required for love to exist. This causes me to trust You all the more.

March 22

I only desire your good. I am always working out plans for your good—even in a painful, fallen world.

"[H]e who began a good work in you will bring it to completion . . ." (Philippians 1:6).

Words of Wisdom

Without freedom there is no love. If it's forced, it's not love. Freedom is not for its own sake, but for the sake of love. Some people believe it's not worth it to be free if it involves this tremendous suffering. All we know is that God doesn't think so. He thinks love is better because He *is* Love.

To do

Think about how the Son of God chose suffering in His passion and death. Think of how much God the Father suffered to watch His Son die. When discussing the problem of evil with others, remind them of these things.

To journal

Always be kind—everyone is fighting a tough battle. Write about the times people were kind to you in your battle, and when you were kind to others.

Prayer

Dear Jesus, earth could be like paradise if we would love each other and carry each other's burdens. Help me do my little part.

March 23

I didn't want to just tell you that I love you. I wanted to show you.

God's Word

"But when the time had fully come, God sent forth his Son, born of woman . . ." (Galatians 4:4).

Words of Wisdom

Jesus is all about tenderness and love and giving Himself to us. Often Jesus is portrayed as something else. His Sacred Heart will help keep us focused on who Jesus really is for us! Just concentrate on His beautiful heart, wounded because of His crazy love for us.

To do

We tend not to believe people who don't "walk the walk." To whom do you need to *show* your love? How will you do that? Do it today.

To journal

We're living in the great drama of salvation history. Write the salvation history of your own life so far. Can you trace your faith back to a person, saint, or culture? (Ultimately trace it back to Jesus and the apostles.) What's your personal experience encountering Jesus and His saving cross?

Prayer

Dear Jesus, You never hold out on us. You give us Your all. Teach me how to be wholehearted in a cynical world.

March 24

Your body is subject to your free will and the free will of others, and since original sin, your body is subject to decay and death. I will always protect your soul if you ask Me to.

God's word

"Do not fear those who kill the body but cannot kill the soul . . ." (Matthew 10:28).

Words of wisdom

One of Jesus's last temptations was to eliminate suffering: "Come down off that cross, and then we will believe in You" (cf. Matthew 27:42). Miracles of protection and healing are real, but they are not guaranteed to anyone.

To do

Look around you and see suffering—man-made and natural. Now is the time to reconcile to this fact. We don't have all the answers because we're not God, but God *has* given us a response to suffering in Jesus.

To journal

God did not protect His own Son from the cross. What have you not been protected from bodily? How has your spirit been protected?

Prayer

Dear Jesus, Satan told You that God would protect You no matter what, but You knew that was not God's true design. Teach me a more radical trust in You than just for bodily safety.

March 25

Often you can bear your own sufferings well enough, but not the sufferings of those you love. You are like My Mother who stood at the foot of My cross.

". . . [S]tanding by the cross of Jesus were his mother . . ." (John 19:25). ". . . [A]nd a sword will pierce through your own soul also" (Luke 2:35). ". . . [T]he world will rejoice; you will be sorrowful, but your sorrow will turn into joy" (John 16:20).

Words of wisdom

We are called to compassion, to suffer with others as Mary did. We are to "rejoice with those who rejoice, weep with those who weep" (Romans 12:15).

To do

Pray the "Hail Holy Queen," or *Mary's Way of the Cross: Walking with the Mother of Jesus*.

To journal

The Church has traditionally spoken of Mary's "Seven Sorrows." What are your seven sorrows? Which sufferings of others move you most to sorrow?

Prayer

Mary, fount of love's devotion, let me share with true emotion all the sorrow you endured (*Stabat Mater*).

March 26

I am risen now as you will be one day. But I also suffer till the end of time in My Mystical Body, that is, in all those who are now suffering.

". . . [T]hat I may know him and the power of his resurrection . . ." (Philippians 3:10).

We live the risen life of Jesus even now, meaning that we can be victorious over sin and transformed in Christ. The fact that we still suffer does not negate the Resurrection.

What are some amazing conversions that you have witnessed or heard about? Ask people to give you their testimonies about how they met God, or how He's working in their lives. How is He working in your life?

When Jesus appeared to Thomas, He still had the wounds from the nails and the spear in His hands and side. These wounds were glorified signs of His love, not a source of pain. At the end of your life, what wounds will be the signs of your love?

Dear Jesus, forgive me for not always believing in the mighty power of Your Resurrection to change me, here and now.

March 27

People claim they want to be free. But often what they want is a perfect world according to their own tastes. They want Me to intervene when they need something fixed, but they want Me to stay out of the rest of their affairs.

God's Word

"Yet you say, 'The way of the Lord is not just.' . . . Is it not your ways that are not just?" (Ezekiel 18:25)

Words of Wisdom

Because of suffering, some people contend that God cannot be all-powerful, all-just, and all-good. They argue that He'd like to help us, but can't. This, of course, is not true. If God kept directly intervening, we wouldn't be free.

To do

Read Luke 13:1–5 (the falling tower of Siloam). What did Jesus say about the bad things that happen to people?

To journal

Have you ever complained "Why me?" about *good* things that happened in your life?

Prayer

Dear Jesus, help me never to abuse my freedom by taking it lightly, or despise my freedom as a responsibility too heavy for me. I want to use my freedom in order to love.

March 28

Do you know what your biggest cross is? It's probably you! Or rather, it is the sin in your life. That's precisely what I came to liberate you from.

God's Word

"[E]rasing the record that stood against us . . . nailing it to the cross" (Colossians 2:14). "And you he made alive, when you were dead through . . . sins" (Ephesians 2:1). "For freedom Christ has set us free" (Galatians 5:1).

Words of Wisdom

It's like our parents told us: Suffering builds character and maturity. And St. Paul tells us that "suffering produces endurance, and endurance produces character, and character produces hope . . ." (Romans 5:3–4).

To do

When G. K. Chesterton was asked, "What's wrong with the world?" he said, "Me." But we don't *have* to be what's wrong with the world! Be the kind of person you'd like to have for a friend.

To journal

It takes a lifetime to be all that a Christian is supposed to be, another Christ. What "crosses of sin" has Jesus already helped you overcome in your life? What's your next challenge?

Prayer

Dear Jesus, I won't ask You to "come down from that cross." There is no other way.

March 29

Where in the New Testament, the New Covenant, did I promise you that you will not suffer? Did I not promise, rather, that you will suffer?

God's word

". . . Christ also suffered for you, leaving you an example, that you should follow in his steps" (1 Peter 2:21).

Words of wisdom

Some people mistakenly think that Jesus suffered and died so we don't have to. But if we are to be perfectly conformed to His image, we have to follow Him in suffering. And we have to suffer with great love, as He suffered, which can make the suffering somehow bearable.

To do

Find New Testament passages that speak about Christians suffering persecution (it started right away!) and how we as Christ's followers are to approach suffering. Read about Vietnamese Cardinal F. X. Nguyen Van Thuan who suffered for thirteen years in a Communist prison.

To journal

What did the French poet Paul Claudel mean when he said: "Jesus did not come to take away suffering, but to fill it with His presence"? Why do Christians act so surprised when they suffer?

Prayer

"Passion of Christ, strengthen me. O good Jesus, hear me. Within Your wounds hide me" (*Anima Christi*).

March 30

Death is natural from a biological point of view. But the death of human beings was not a part of My original plan. Death entered the world through sin. So death is unnatural.

God's Word

". . . [T]he day that you eat of it you shall die" (Genesis 2:17).
". . . God did not make death . . ." (Wisdom 1:13).

Words of wisdom

The cross is inevitable, at the very least, when we face our own death. Even if we have a sudden, painless death, we know that death is approaching, and when we die, we will face the biggest transition of our existence.

To do

Think and talk with God about your own death. Search online or in a Catholic prayer book for a prayer for a happy death.

To journal

We live at three life-levels simultaneously: natural (care for our bodies), human (care for our personal relationships), and supernatural (care for our souls and relationship with God). Where are you strongest? Where are you weakest?

Prayer

Dear Jesus, the Tohono O'Odham Nation of Mission San Xavier del Bac, Arizona, have a beautiful maze-like symbol depicting how we must go through many trials in life and accept our own death. Give me this understanding, acceptance, and peace.

March 31

You will die as I did. But all other evils in your life have been overcome already—all you need to do is claim My redemption in your life.

God's Word

"The last enemy to be destroyed is death" (1 Corinthians 15:26). ". . . [A]nd I, when I am lifted up from the earth, will draw all men to myself" (John 12:32).

Words of Wisdom

When St. Edith Stein was going to her death in the gas chamber at Auschwitz she quoted the Easter hymn, "Vexilla Regis": "Hail, O Cross, our only hope." We should take courage from those who do not waver in their faith, even in the face of death.

To do

Read through the words of Easter hymns from a hymnal. Do you believe these words? What do they mean for your life? Read *The Suffering of Love: Christ's Descent into the Hell of Human Hopelessness* by Regis Martin.

To journal

Christopher West says: "Jesus didn't come to give us more laws, but to change our hearts." What does this mean?

Prayer

"Christ the Victor-Giant quells the foe defiant. Let the ransomed people sing: Glory to our Easter King! Alleluia! Alleluia!"

April 1

What was the very first sin of Adam and Eve in the Garden of Eden?
Disobedience? No. It was to be suspicious of My Father.

"It is better to take refuge in the LORD than to put confidence in princes" (Psalm 118:9).

When have I taken things into my own hands (without God)? When did I trust God even when it seemed counterintuitive? What were the outcomes?

Each of us is born into a particular culture and historical reality. What are the "signs of the times" that motivate you to improve the world? What are you going to do about this call?

In *The Lay Members of Christ's Faithful People*, Pope John Paul II suggests these ways to discern God's will: "a receptive listening to the Word of God and the Church, fervent and constant prayer, recourse to a wise and loving spiritual guide, and a faithful discernment of the gifts and talents given by God. . . ." How you are discerning each of these ways?

Dear Jesus, I have trust issues. I guess we all do. Help me learn to step out in faith more and more.

April 2

So, what is My will? My will is that we be united forever in love. Everything else falls into place around this fact.

God's word

"For this is the will of God, your sanctification . . ." (1 Thessalonians 4:3).

Words of wisdom

There are so many false teachings about God and what His will is. Many claim to speak for Him. But if they do not speak first about the fact that God loves us and makes it very possible for us to do His will, they are certainly not speaking for Him.

To do

The next time you're in a quandary about what God's will might be, fix your eyes on heaven—God's ultimate will and your ultimate goal—in order to get clarity.

To journal

What are some inaccuracies you have heard about the will of God? Has anyone ever approached you and said, "God told me to tell you . . . ?" If so, do you think what they said was authentic? Why or why not?

Prayer

Dear Jesus, everything You do is for my ultimate good and happiness. You don't dish out "cheap grace." I thank You for this, because I want the real thing.

April 3

You can know My will through reason and revelation. Everything that comes from Me, everything that is touched by Me, everything that belongs to Me, speaks of Me.

God's Word

"The LORD has bared his holy arm . . . and all the ends of the earth shall see the salvation of our God" (Isaiah 52:10).

Words of Wisdom

God has given us three "books" of revelation. God the Father, our Creator, gives us creation as our first book of revelation. God the Son, our Redeemer, is the Word who reveals Himself in Sacred Scripture. God the Holy Spirit, our Sanctifier, is active in the Sacred Tradition of the Church. We are well provided for with these amazing treasures!

To Do

Search an online Bible for the phrase: "will of God." What did you discover?

To Journal

The Bible and Church teachings express God's will for us. What Scripture or Church teaching is giving you direction in your life right now?

Prayer

Dear Jesus, You have given us so many helps to know Your will— "what is good and acceptable and perfect" (Romans 12:2). Sometimes I forget the answers are all around me.

April 4

Do you enjoy nature? I made it all for you. I am constantly communicating My love and My plans for you through the material world.

God's Word

"Since the creation of the world his invisible nature . . . has been clearly perceived in the things that have been made" (Romans 1:20).

Words of Wisdom

Do you get blissfully "lost" in nature? Try to remember who it's all from! Do you dislike being outside in varying weather, preferring the indoors and the "concrete jungle"? Try to get back in touch with nature! It has much to tell you.

To Do

Spend some time praying with nature. Don't only enjoy it, but really "listen" and "read" what God is saying to us and to you personally through nature.

To Journal

Write down your favorite natural wonders. What has God revealed to you about Himself and His will through them? What have you learned about yourself through them?

Prayer

Dear Jesus, thank You for the beauty and simplicity of nature. Let it always delight me, heal me, and lead me to You!

April 5

My written word is your sure guide. It is enlightenment, consolation, and most of all, My love letter to you.

God's word

"Thy word is a lamp to my feet and a light to my path" (Psalm 119:105).

God is always communicating. Always. If we can't hear Him, perhaps we need to open our ears a little more! Perhaps we don't like what He says and so we look for a different word from Him. Thus, He seems silent. The Apostle John says that all the books in the world couldn't hold what God has done (and is doing and saying right now)!

to do

St. Jerome once said, "Ignorance of the Scripture is ignorance of Christ." Read the Bible daily. Join a Catholic Bible study or do one on your own.

to journal

". . . I know the plans I have for you . . . to give you a future and a hope" (Jeremiah 29:11). What clues do you have from God's word about your future?

Prayer

Dear Jesus, even Your "hard sayings" are good news because they have the power to heal and redeem me. Help me always experience Your word as good, helping me see the big picture.

April 6

My Church is so misunderstood. It is seen as a purely human, bureaucratic organization, but it is My Mystical Body. It is Me continuing My mission in the world.

God's Word

"He who hears you hears me, and he who rejects you rejects me . . ." (Luke 10:16).

Words of Wisdom

The Catholic Church was willed, instituted, and constituted by Christ, and although she is made up of human beings, she is guided by the Holy Spirit. We have to be careful not to confuse the sinful actions of individual Catholics—even priests and bishops—with the actual holiness of the Church.

To do

Read numbers 748–972 in the *Catechism of the Catholic Church* on the Catholic Church. Why was Mary included in this part of the Catechism (nos. 963–972)?

To journal

When we say the Creed, we say: I *believe* in the Catholic Church. This means there is an element of mystery to the Church, otherwise, we would not profess faith in it. What mystery of the Church do you wrestle with? What mystery do you love?

Prayer

Dear Jesus, thank You for the Church. Help me love her, understand her, and be able to explain her to others.

April 7

What is My will for you, specifically? Talk to Me. Listen to Me. You can know My will through prayer.

God's word

"As a deer longs for flowing streams, so my soul longs for you, O God" (Psalm 42:1 NRSV).

Words of wisdom

If you read through the Acts of the Apostles, you'll see that when God gave the apostles a directive, it was often when they were at prayer. Prayer preceded and accompanied all important decisions, as well as taking counsel with wise and holy people.

To do

If you didn't start this book from the beginning, go back and read through February, which is all about prayer. Or, if you read it already, go back and review.

To journal

Write about some times you prayed to know God's will and felt His guidance to go one way or the other, confirmation of what you were doing, or an impetus to change direction?

Prayer

Dear Jesus, Your care is ongoing. You are closer to me than I am to myself. I cannot be ahead of You or behind You because You are right with me.

April 8

Do you think you know what your vocation in life is? I have put certain desires in your heart. What do you feel most called to be?

God's word

". . . [T]he LORD was not in the wind . . . earthquake . . . fire. . . . [A]fter the fire there was a tiny whispering sound" (1 Kings 19:11, 12 NAB).

Words of wisdom

God gently invites us, but always leaves us free. This is not a kind of passive-aggressiveness, with God only pretending to respect our freedom. God truly respects our freedom. Love must respond freely.

To do

If we are wise, we'll turn to God to help us, even in our response to Him. God asks in accord with the desires He has planted in our hearts. There's a saying: "God will not send us to the missions without first putting the missions in our heart."

To journal

Mother Paula of the Daughters of St. Paul encouraged her sisters to "return love for love." How would you respond to her question: "God has given you your very life. What are you going to do for Him?"

Prayer

Dear Jesus, help me know what You've placed in my heart; help me to hear Your invitations and to respond wholeheartedly with love.

April 9

Your first vocation is to love as I love, to make a total gift of yourself. Will you do this as a religious, married, or single woman? This is a call and a choice we work out together.

God's word

"For he has made known to us in all wisdom and insight the mystery of his will . . ." (Ephesians 1:9).

Words of wisdom

Everyone in the world has the exact same vocation: to love. Your greatest accomplishment in life will be how you love. We often take pride in our careers, but really, it's relationships that matter most.

To do

Discerning your vocation requires help. Find a spiritual director or mentor who values all three vocations.

To journal

Henri Nouwen said that reflecting the glimpse of God uniquely given us is our first vocation. How do you see yourself as a reflection of that uniqueness?

Prayer

Dear Jesus, although I'm called to deny myself and follow You, that doesn't mean my vocation has to be the life I consider hardest. Help me understand that hardest is not the best. The best vocation is the one I'm called to follow.

April 10

I am the spouse of every soul I have created, but is this reality so tangible to you, so fulfilling, that I could be your one and only, your true love?

"One thing have I asked of the LORD . . . that I may dwell in the house of the LORD all the days of my life, to behold the beauty of the LORD . . . " (Psalm 27:4).

Words of Wisdom

Religious life is not always understood or appreciated, even by Catholics. Be patient with those who don't understand.

To do

Visit some religious congregations that you feel drawn to because of their specific spirituality and mission. Attend vocational discernment retreats to discover what religious life is all about. Check out the websites of various congregations included throughout this book.

To journal

What type of religious communities could you imagine yourself joining? Why?

Prayer

Dear Jesus, You created the human heart, so You know best how to fill it. I will trust You if You're calling me to religious life. Give me courage to overcome obstacles that others, even those closest to me, might put in my way.

April 11

Most people choose marriage as their vocation. If you feel called to marriage, begin praying now for your future spouse. I am the best dating service.

God's Word

"It is not good that the man should be alone . . ." (Genesis 2:18).

Words of Wisdom

You're taking advice from a nun on marriage? You must be desperate! Seriously, *don't* be desperate about getting married. Although it doesn't feel like it, you have plenty of time. Just keep praying and doing all the right things. Don't compromise. Don't settle. Have faith like the women of the Bible.

To do

Begin studying Pope John Paul II's theology of the body—the best marriage preparation ever! If you already have a boyfriend, study together! Read *Wait for Me* by Rebecca Saint James for practical ways to prepare for marriage.

To journal

What are you looking for in a spouse? Be careful of making laundry lists of attributes. Let God surprise you with the whole person! What steps are you taking to prepare for a beautiful marriage?

Prayer

Dear Jesus, Mary, and Joseph, if I'm called to marriage, help my future spouse and I to embrace true married and family life in its fullness.

April 12

Do you feel that you're not called to marriage or religious life? That is still a call. Everyone is called because no one is created to be truly alone.

God's Word

"For whoever would save his life will lose it, and whoever loses his life for my sake will find it" (Matthew 16:25).

Words of Wisdom

"Serving God through vowed commitment is the highlight of my life. It is the reason for getting up in the morning and praising God through ministry to others." (Sr. Magdala Marie Gilbert, OSP, www.oblatesisters.com)

To Do

If you feel you want to live a *consecrated* single life, look into Third Orders, secular institutes, or consecrated virginity. If not, consider how you will make a gift of self in your single life.

To journal

If religious are misunderstood, how much more are single people! What are typical comments that show incomprehension of the single vocation? How can you respond?

Prayer

Dear Jesus, I'm single for now, but I don't know if that will continue. Help me accept in peace and joy my singlehood, and if it becomes clear this is my vocation, help me embrace it and live it to the full.

April 13

I have already consecrated you to Myself in Baptism. Whatever state of life you choose, you will be living out your Baptism.

God's word

"Do you not know that all of us who have been baptized into Christ Jesus were baptized into his death?" (Romans 6:3)

Words of Wisdom

God doesn't call the equipped; He equips the called. Stay open to whatever adventure the Lord may have in store for you. Be sure to learn about all three states of life so you can make an informed decision.

To do

Check out these books on discernment: *Discernment: Acquiring the Heart of God* by Marko Ivan Rupnik, *What Does God Want?* by Michael Scanlan, *Authenticity: A Biblical Theology of Discernment* by Thomas Dubay, *LifeWork: Finding Purpose in Your Life* by Rick Sarkisian.

To journal

Although God gives us certain desires, talents, and abilities, He sometimes stretches us. What are some ways God has already stretched you to do and be what you never thought possible?

Prayer

Dear Jesus, You and I are going to work out this vocation thing together. Sometimes it feels like the agony in the garden, sometimes I feel my will wrestling with Yours, however, "not my will, but thine, be done" (Luke 22:42).

April 14

Do you find discerning your vocation difficult? Do you find discerning My will difficult in general? Trust Me. I am not hiding or playing games with you.

God's Word

"For God is not a God of confusion but of peace . . ." (1 Corinthians 14:33).

Words of Wisdom

A young woman struggling to discern her vocation said: "I wouldn't wish discernment on anyone!" Discernment is universally an intense, foggy, time-consuming experience—and maybe it's supposed to be that way! Why? Perhaps so that we focus, realize how important the decision we're about to make is, and take time to decide well. If we falter in our decision later on, we can remember and retrace the whole process.

To do

In whatever you're discerning now, ask yourself: What brings me true peace? Take note of when you experience peace. Follow the peace.

To journal

Discernment is like transition because it's about change. Most of us don't like too much change. Think of some transitions you've already been through. What helped you?

Prayer

Dear Jesus, if nothing else, discernment teaches me patience. Help me to learn from the whole process.

April 15

Are you anxious about knowing My will? Don't be. Your desire to know and do My will is already pleasing to Me.

God's Word

"Teach me to do your will . . ." (Psalm 143:10 NRSV).

Words of Wisdom

Doing God's will is not only about "following our hearts." We need to be serious about studying good philosophy and theology so that we have spiritual wealth to draw on to help ourselves and others.

To Do

Sometimes making a list of pros and cons can bring things into sharp relief. Try posing a direct question to God in prayer: "Should I . . . ?" See if something stirs in your heart. Don't ask advice of too many people because you'll get too many different answers!

To Journal

At a certain point, the voices of various angels and saints that Joan of Arc could hear went silent. She had to go by what she already knew and choose in the dark. Write about a time you had to "choose in the dark."

Prayer

Dear Jesus, I am so amazed that, after forming my conscience and character according to You and the Church, You trust me to make good choices. Let me know when I'm mistaken and turn me around.

April 16

Discerning your vocation is just the beginning. You'll need constant discernment for living out your vocation.

God's word

"Trust in the LORD . . . do not rely on your own insight" (Proverbs 3:5).

Words of wisdom

Discernment is a way of life. It is a way of keeping in touch with God and letting Him guide your life. Discernment is God's clever way of getting us to pray more!

To do

In *What Does God Want?*, Fr. Michael Scanlan offers five "C's" of discernment: Is it in *conformity* with the already-known will of God? Does it lead me to *conversion*? Is it *consistent* with the way God has been leading me? What *confirmation* have I received? Is it a *conviction* of my heart?

To journal

Even though we've found Truth Himself, we need to be active seekers of how God's truth applies to our lives and world. Write out these lines by James Russell Lowell: "New occasions teach new duties / time makes ancient good uncouth. / They must upward still and onwards / who would keep abreast of truth."

Prayer

Dear Jesus, don't let me become complacent, but ever more awake and alive to You and to all truth.

April 17

Always remember that your first vocation is to love. Don't worry about what form this will take. I may have a mission in mind for you, but you are not a functionary, you are a person.

God's Word

"But strive first for the kingdom of God and his righteousness, and all these things will be given to you as well" (Matthew 6:33 NRSV).

Words of wisdom

God isn't waiting for us to get His will exactly right or we'll blow it. Life is not that precise. Life is an ebb and flow. The important thing is that we seek and do His will as best we can. Our vocation is about our ongoing relationship with God, not a category that we put ourselves in.

To do

When difficulties arise in our state of life, we shouldn't immediately rush to re-discern our calling. Problems are to be resolved, and crosses to be borne *within* our vocation. A vocation is a serious commitment.

To journal

Write about a time you resolved a problem within your family, place of work, school, team, etc. without quitting.

Prayer

Dear Jesus, every way of life has its own crosses and joys. Grant me holy perseverance in the life to which I am called.

April 18

You are My work of art. The more you submit to My masterful touch, the more beautiful you'll be.

God's word

"You did not choose me, but I chose you . . ." (John 15:16).

Words of wisdom

The signs of a religious vocation might be the following (or not!): you always want *more* out of life; you are drawn to prayer and service; you know you could live happily without marriage; people mention religious vocation to you and you see it as a possibility, whereas many young women don't; you're genuinely attracted to that way of life; the thought won't go away; you find yourself in "eternity mode"—you just can't seem to hold onto things that are passing.

To do

Mother Teresa saw herself as a little pencil in God's hand. Try to get an image of yourself in God's hands.

To journal

Hans Christian Andersen said: "God writes a fairytale with the life of every person." (If you read his original fairytales, they're not all rosy!) What is the fairytale of your life?

Prayer

Dear Jesus, You know which state of life I'll be happiest and most fruitful in. Just let me know.

April 19

Are you afraid of being alone, of being lonely in life? That is not My plan for you or anyone. If you are making a gift of yourself, you'll never be alone.

God's word

". . . [T]here is no one who has left house or brothers or sisters or mother or father or children or lands, for my sake and for the gospel, who will not receive a hundredfold now in this time . . . with persecutions, and in the age to come eternal life" (Mark 10:29–30).

Words of wisdom

"You think you're doing such a great thing when you give everything to God, but He turns around and gives it all right back to you!" (Sr. Patricia Mary Maresca, FSP, www.daughtersofstpaul.org)

To do

Every person, even those called to the single life, is also called to some form of community. Join a community beyond family, work, school, and church.

To journal

The Prayer of St. Francis says "in giving we receive." When is a time you thought you were giving, but were really receiving much more?

Prayer

Dear Jesus, help me to understand that often I have to take the first step, and not just wait for things to happen.

April 20

Do you have goals and dreams? Excellent. Where do you think they came from?

God's Word

"[T]o everyone who has will more be given, and he will have abundance . . ." (Matthew 25:29).

Words of Wisdom

"Let His Holy Spirit fill you with courage and confidence to become the unique gift you are meant to be, in any circumstance, with any group of people." (Sr. Mary Gabriel Devlin, SV, www.sistersoflife.org)

To do

Read *Man's Search for Meaning* by Viktor Frankl. What does the author say is the last of the human freedoms? What does he say we are always able to choose in any situation?

To journal

Write out some of your short- and long-term goals and dreams. How will you attain them? What if your life takes a drastic turn away from these goals and dreams? Think now of how you will respond.

Prayer

Dear Jesus, I know You approve of my having goals and dreams. But life is wild and woolly, and hard work and determination do *not* guarantee success. As I plan and dream, keep me open to the fact that much of life is not in my control. Help me be prepared for anything.

April 21

Are you concerned that your intentions are not completely pure? Don't be afraid. Human beings have mixed motives. Purification is a lifelong process. Begin where you are.

God's Word

"One there is who is good" (Matthew 19:17). "We also are men, of like nature with you . . ." (Acts 14:15).

Words of Wisdom

"Relax, O chosen one! God loves you completely, cherishing your every step on your journey to Him. Hasten to Him with open arms. All He wants is your love." (Sr. Fintan Keaveney, CSN, www.nazarethhouse.org)

To do

Try to get to the root of your motives for doing something that you freely choose to do. They're complex, aren't they? It's good to reflect and examine your conscience daily, but you will always remain a bit of a mystery to yourself.

To journal

Write about a time you felt your intention was very pure. Did you feel God's grace impelling you from within and without?

Prayer

". . . I do what I do not want. . . . I do not do the good I want. . . . Who will deliver me from this body of death? Thanks be to God through Jesus Christ our Lord!" (Romans 7:16, 19, 24–25)

April 22

Are you looking for a sign from Me? I am pleased that you desire to know and do My will, but I may choose not to give you a sign.

"This generation is an evil generation; it seeks a sign . . ." (Luke 11:29).

Words of wisdom

God primarily works through ordinary means: people, events, opportunities, circumstances, natural inclinations and abilities, intuitions, and inspirations. There are two ways of looking at this: Either everything is miraculous or nothing is miraculous. (Both, because God is so amazing!)

To do

Always asking God for special, personal signs can show a lack of spiritual maturity, or a lack of trust in what He has already revealed. Focus on ways you can know God's will about personal and other matters without special signs.

To journal

The Church's Magisterium is a big help to knowing God's will, but did you know that most matters of faith don't have to be declared dogmas because they are part of the ordinary Magisterium? In other words, the Church has always held and taught certain things. What are some ordinary parts of our faith that you find extraordinary?

Prayer

Dear Jesus, thanks for the extraordinary ordinary.

April 23

Humanity has always sought to know My will. But there are no formulas to know Me—there is only our loving relationship.

God's word

"There shall not be found among you . . . any one who practises divination, a soothsayer, or an augur, or a sorcerer, or a charmer, or a medium . . ." (Deuteronomy 18:10–11).

Words of wisdom

Unfortunately, many attempts to know the will of God are really attempts to know and control the future, other people, or even God. God forbids this. We are not supposed to know or be in control of these things; the future is not determined ahead of time; and the power used in these attempts might be real, but not of God.

To do

If you have taken part in witchcraft, Wicca, fortune-telling, Ouija boards, tarot cards, psychic readings, séances, Satanism, horoscopes, etc., bring it to Confession. Also admonish friends who dabble in the occult (see *Catechism of the Catholic Church*, nos. 2110–2117).

To journal

God has given us His final Word: Jesus. Jesus is all we need. Write a poem or love-letter to Jesus about His sufficiency in your life.

Prayer

Dear Jesus, prayer is the answer to knowing Your will. There is no substitute for prayer.

April 24

My will is not something separate from Me, something out there that you must acquire; just like salvation is not a thing, but our relationship!

God's Word

"I fed you with milk, not solid food; for you were not ready for it; and even yet you are not ready . . ." (1 Corinthians 3:2).

Words of Wisdom

Special signs can be difficult to interpret. A professed sister on the East Coast prayed for snow in late May as a sign that she should join another congregation. A freak storm brought six inches of snow, so she joined the other congregation. Within three months, she returned to her former community.

To do

Following the daily Scripture readings from Mass is a great way to read the Bible. However, the whole Bible is not contained in the liturgy—so be sure to try to read the whole book!

To journal

Are you superstitious? Do you "Bible-crack" (randomly open the Bible), expecting God to direct you? God can work through anything, but remember, the Bible is not a gigantic fortune cookie.

Prayer

Dear Jesus, help me educate myself in Scripture and Church teaching as a source of Your true knowledge and wisdom for my life.

April 25

I have spoken to My people in dreams, but I may choose to speak to you differently.

God's Word

". . . [I]n these last days he has spoken to us by a Son . . ." (Hebrews 1:2).

Words of Wisdom

The subconscious is a fascinating area of study. Many cultures, like those of Native Americans, believed that God (or gods) speaks in dreams. If this is not part of your culture, it will be harder for you to interpret what God might be saying through dreams. We know that dreams are also a way the brain processes the day.

To Do

It is much easier to be aware of our conscious moments—and there is much to deal with there! What are some problems, conundrums, and questions your *conscious* mind is turning over lately? Take these to prayer.

To Journal

Have you had significant or poignant dreams? Do you think God was speaking to you through them? What was He saying? Have your dreams ever revealed something going on deep inside of you "below the surface?"

Prayer

Dear Jesus, however you want to communicate with me is just fine. "Speak, LORD, for your servant is listening" (1 Samuel 3:9 NRSV).

April 26

Don't forget My often neglected gifts of reason and common sense.

God's word

"For which of you, desiring to build a tower, does not first . . . count the cost . . . ?" (Luke 14:28) "If you love me, you will keep my commandments" (John 14:15).

Words of wisdom

"To obey is better than sacrifice" (1 Samuel 15:22), but God doesn't want blind obedience. Grace builds on nature, and God doesn't want us to shut off the brain He gave us! We'll be able to serve Him and His people better if we use our intelligence.

To do

If you faint at the sight of blood, you probably shouldn't become a nurse! Think of some things you absolutely know you're not called to and cross them off your list of possible life-paths or careers.

To journal

In seeking the will of God, have you gone overboard? Have you over-spiritualized and overcomplicated things? How can you uncomplicate them?

Prayer

Dear Jesus, You must laugh sometimes at our crazy spiritual contortions! Spouses know each other's will—often without words. Let me be that close to You.

April 27

You can trust Me, but I'm not "safe" in the sense that I can be put in a box. And I won't let you be in a box either. I will always call you higher, even as you advance in age.

God's word

"Where were you when I laid the foundation of the earth? Tell me, if you have understanding" (Job 38:4).

Words of wisdom

The wildest and safest place to be is the will of God. ". . . [N]o one is able to snatch them out of the Father's hand" (John 10:29). Sometimes life with God can seem chaotic, but He's teaching us to let go.

To do

Relationships have phases. God doesn't change, but we do. Can you decipher phases in your relationship with God? Give these phases names. Read Hannah Hurnard's classic, *Hinds' Feet on High Places*, an allegory on following God.

To journal

Just when we think we understand something, master something, get comfortable, God seems to change it up on us. When have you felt this happen in your life?

Prayer

Dear Jesus, you said, "Follow Me." This implies movement. Keep me going when I get stuck.

April 28

Does My will seem too difficult for you? I know you are afraid, but do not be afraid.

God's Word

"In hope he believed against hope . . ." (Romans 4:18).

Words of Wisdom

Have you ever thought: What's God going to do to me if I give Him all? Is He going to ask too much? God loves us so much that He only has one mode: All. We humans like to hold back and hedge our bets.

To Do

Part of trust is risk. If you can get to eighty percent sure about your vocation in life, go for it! (If you can get to eighty percent sure about anything besides death, taxes, and God's love, go for it!) God wants us to exercise our willpower, so that we can gain wisdom through experience, and trust Him even more. Act on what you believe is your vocation.

To Journal

What are you most afraid of when it comes to doing God's will? When have you risked in faith? How did it turn out?

Prayer

Dear Jesus, I'm amazed that I can negotiate with You. Thank You for Your patience as I give You all of myself, little by little.

April 29

My will is not always something outside of you. It can be a part of who you are!

"But the word is very near you; it is in your mouth and in your heart, so that you can do it" (Deuteronomy 30:14). "Reflect upon what has been assigned to you, for you do not need what is hidden" (Sirach 3:22).

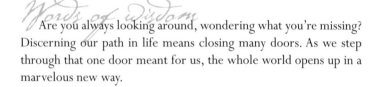

Words of wisdom

Are you always looking around, wondering what you're missing? Discerning our path in life means closing many doors. As we step through that one door meant for us, the whole world opens up in a marvelous new way.

To do

Get in the habit of praying the Angelus three times a day (morning, noon, and night). That way you will be repeating Mary's words often: "Let it be to me according to your word" (Luke 1:38).

To journal

How can you submit more to the will of God? Write out Philippians 2:5–11, which is called the "Carmen Christi" or "Song of Christ." What did Jesus become?

Prayer

Dear Jesus, help me to pray and discern with my whole being. Help me to "test everything; hold fast what is good" (1 Thessalonians 5:21).

April 30

Do I know the future—your future? Yes, because I am outside of time. All time is present to Me: past, present, and future.

"Our God is in the heavens; he does whatever he pleases" (Psalm 115:3).

Some people think that because God knows the future, we are somehow predetermined, that God is *making us* choose a certain way, or that we really don't have free will. This is fatalism, and nothing could be more untrue.

Watch a river. God is working the way a river flows on, but we are always free to work with Him or not. Are you treading water? Cross-cutting the river? Swimming upstream? Sitting on the bank? Holding on to the side? Going with God's flow?

There's a wonderful word that describes God: ineffable. It means "too overpowering to be expressed in words, unutterable, indefinable." What are some things about God that you find ineffable?

Dear Jesus, I'm so glad to know that You are doing whatever You will. That's a good thing because You are Truth, Beauty, Goodness, and Love itself!

May 1

If life is all about love, that means life is all about relationships. I am all about relationships because my Father, the Holy Spirit, and I are a Trinity of Divine Persons eternally loving each other.

God's Word

"Let us make man in our image . . ." (Genesis 1:26). ". . . [H]e saw the Spirit of God descending like a dove, and alighting on him; and lo, a voice from heaven saying, 'This is my beloved Son, with whom I am well pleased'" (Matthew 3:16–17).

Words of Wisdom

Without Jesus, we would never have known that God is a Trinity. Keep your eyes fixed on Jesus and He will reveal everything to you.

To do

Can't get your mind around the Trinity? Neither could some of the greatest saints like St. Augustine who wrote about the Trinity. But that doesn't mean we shouldn't try to understand God more. St. Anselm called theology "faith seeking understanding." Always have a curious faith.

To journal

Write out your understandings, explanations, and questions about the Trinity.

Prayer

Dear Jesus, if I understood You, and the Father, and the Holy Spirit, You wouldn't be God. Help me to live with the *mystery* of You!

May 2

When you were baptized you were given a share in My divine life. You know it as sanctifying grace. You are sharing in the love of the Trinity!

God's word

". . . [N]o one knows who the Son is except the Father, or who the Father is except the Son and any one to whom the Son chooses to reveal him" (Luke 10:22).

Words of Wisdom

Joan of Arc was asked if she was in a state of grace (something no one can answer with absolute certainty). She answered: "If I am, I thank God. If I am not, I pray that God will put me there." Carefully preserve and grow in your relationship with God which should mean *everything*.

To do

The only thing that can disrupt your relationship with the Trinity is sin. Trace out the history of your relationship with God.

To journal

Love is something we reach out and *give*, not something we *get*. But we will also get love because others will reach out in love to us! What are you doing to grow in love?

Prayer

Dear Jesus, help me focus on the giving of love, not the *getting*, but let me rejoice in both.

May 3

My family is the Trinity, which I invite the entire human family to participate in. All people are My children because I am the source of life, but they must accept to have my divine life in them.

God's Word

"For we are indeed his offspring" (Acts 17:28).

Words of Wisdom

"Look to St. Francis for a clue to the secret of happiness—a life of joy as part of God's family, with God as your Father who loves you totally, Jesus as your brother who gave His life for you, and Mary as your mother who will always intercede for you." (Sr. M. Lois DeLee, OSF, www.ssfpa.org)

To do

People have a *right* to know about Jesus and His invitation to participate in the Trinity. Their response is personal, but we must find a way to invite them!

To journal

Everyone can do something to witness to God's greatness, goodness, and love in their lives. What can you do? What are you doing?

Prayer

Dear Jesus, help me find simple, real ways to invite others to You. People need You.

May 4

My human family—which participates in My divine life—is the Church. Do you love My Church?

God's Word

". . . [T]hat he might present the church to himself in splendour, without spot or wrinkle or any such thing, that she might be holy and without blemish" (Ephesians 5:27).

Words of Wisdom

The Church on earth is the pilgrim Church, the Church in purgatory is the Church being purified for heaven, the Church in heaven is the blessed sharing in Jesus's glory and His victory over sin and death. All together we are the "communion of saints" and the "Mystical Body of Christ," able to help one another through prayer and acts of charity.

To do

Ask yourself what kind of member of the Church you are. Do you need to be more prayerful, more involved, more serving? How?

To journal

Write about your relationship and attitude toward the Church. Are there aspects of the Church you struggle with? What are you doing to resolve the struggle?

Prayer

Dear Jesus, You love the Church and gave Yourself up for her. Help me to love the Church as You do.

May 5

Your life on this earth is a gift and a journey, but also a battle to be fought against sin, the devil, and all that is in the world that is against Me and against human beings.

God's word

". . . [T]he LORD saves not with sword and spear; for the battle is the LORD's . . ." (1 Samuel 17:47).

Words of wisdom

Periods in our lives can be smooth sailing, but generally, we are engaged in a constant effort against temptation. The saints tell us that if we remain unperturbed for too long, it's either a special grace, or Satan considers us no threat!

To do

What tools do you use to fight your spiritual battles? (cf. Ephesians 6:10–18) The ordinary means are: prayer, examination of conscience, Confession, Eucharist, acts of charity, almsgiving, and sacramentals. These are also preventative means that keep us spiritually healthy!

To journal

Do you feel life is a battle? How? What are your specific battles? What are your wounds? (Wounds are badges of honor that show we're not sitting on the sidelines!)

Prayer

"Soul of Christ, sanctify me. Body of Christ, save me. Blood of Christ, inebriate me. Water from the side of Christ, wash me." (*Anima Christi*)

May 6

The holy souls in purgatory are dear to Me. They suffer because they are not yet in heaven with Me. Will you help them with prayer and sacrifices?

God's word

". . . [H]e made atonement for the dead, that they might be delivered from their sin" (2 Maccabees 12:45).

Words of Wisdom

God does not send anyone to purgatory. The soul knows it is not ready to see God and willingly undergoes purification. Probably the majority of us will need this purification and time of transition.

To do

Make a list of deceased people to pray for. Include the unidentified, forgotten souls.

To journal

The pain of purgatory is acute because it involves a certain separation from God after seeing Him and being in His loving presence after death, but those in purgatory have the joy of knowing they're going to heaven. Have you thought of purgatory in these terms before? If not, how does this change the thought of your own death?

Prayer

"Eternal rest grant unto them, O Lord, and let perpetual light shine upon them."

May 7

Life is so short. Live it well. Trust in Me, and you'll join Me, My saints, and your loved ones in heaven where love and all good things eternally increase.

God's Word

"I have fought the good fight, I have finished the race, I have kept the faith" (2 Timothy 4:7).

Words of Wisdom

The existential philosopher, Jean-Paul Sartre, said: "Hell is other people." But so is heaven! Hell may be other *nasty* people, but heaven is other *wonderful* people!

To do

All depictions and descriptions of heaven (books, movies, paintings, etc.) fall miserably short, and can have the opposite effect of turning us *off*, when heaven should be the most attractive thing ever! Describe your imaginings of heaven to someone else.

To journal

How do I feel about other people? Sometimes we don't like other people, social gatherings, etc., because they don't reflect God's unconditional love. Write about the kind of people and social gatherings that would be a foretaste of heaven.

Prayer

Dear Jesus, I, too, am responsible to be Your body, Your Church, welcoming everyone. Help me practice hospitality wherever I am, so that I can create a little bit of heaven on earth.

May 8

There are many who worship and follow Me as Christians. They are your brothers and sisters in a special way. Even if they reject you, do not reject them. One day their eyes will be open to the fullness of truth.

God's Word

"And I have other sheep, that are not of this fold; I must bring them also, and they will heed my voice. So there shall be one flock, one shepherd" (John 10:16).

Words of Wisdom

Be sure to ground yourself well in your Catholic Christian faith before engaging in ecumenical dialogue. Many of our Protestant brothers and sisters are strong in their faith and trained in evangelism/proselytizing. (If only *we* were as prepared and convincing!)

To Do

Learn about the various Christian denominations, when and how they started, who started them, and what they believe.

To Journal

What have your faith-encounters with non-Catholic Christians been like? Describe how you want to go about them in the future. How do you and your Protestant friends enjoy being Christians together?

Prayer

Dear Jesus, I pray with You in Your high priestly prayer "that they may all be one" (John 17:21). Amen.

May 9

All people are My children. Some religions and beliefs are closer to the total truth about Me, some are further away. Appreciate the truth found in the teachings of other religions and always respect all my children.

God's word

"And this is eternal life, that they know thee" (John 17:3).

Words of Wisdom

Always remember that we have a special relationship with the Jewish faith. It is not just one religion among many, but God's Chosen People through whom He has blessed the whole world in Jesus! They are our "root" (cf. Romans 11:18). Christianity is the continuum of Judaism and salvation history. We are the New Israel, participants in the New Covenant foretold by Jeremiah.

To do

Join a Catholic Bible study group or use www.biblestudyforcatholics.com. Read *Salvation Is from the Jews* by Roy Schoeman, *A Father Who Keeps His Promises* by Scott Hahn, *The Promise* by Jean-Marie Lustiger, or anything by Abraham Heschel.

To journal

How would you describe the difference between a religion and a cult? How would you respond to someone who claims that all religions are cults?

Prayer

Dear Jesus, may all come to know You, and may I always honor the attempts of others to seek Your face.

May 10

Do you have a loving family? They can give you a great head-start in life and be one of your greatest supports. But as an individual you are also loved by and belong first of all to Me.

God's Word

". . . [Jesus] went down with them [Mary and Joseph] and came to Nazareth, and was obedient to them . . ." (Luke 2:51).

Words of Wisdom

Families are great, but nobody can push your buttons like your own family. That just shows how close you really are.

To Do

The family is the first school of love, the domestic church, the fundamental cell of society. What can you do to strengthen the life of your family? What is your relationship like with each member of your family? Do something today to improve one of these relationships.

To Journal

What hereditary gifts do you have from your family? What learned gifts do you have from them? Describe the "give and take" in your family. Do you do more giving or taking?

Prayer

Dear Jesus, thank You for Your plan for humanity called families. The family is under attack today because it's so important. Help us uphold the sanctity of families and family life.

May 11

Do you have an unloving family? This can be one of your life's greatest hurts and hurdles. But remember, you are Mine.

God's Word

". . . [S]wear to me by the LORD that you in turn will deal kindly with my family" (Joshua 2:12 NRSV).

Words of Wisdom

It takes a long time to unravel and understand what happened to us in our families. Good and bad are so closely enmeshed. And families are famous for secrets that we may not know right away. One thing families show us is that we are meant for true communion, and we won't settle for anything less.

To Do

Are you working on forgiving your parents or family members? Adoptive family? Guardian(s)? This may be your life's task. Wouldn't it be nice to finish early? Plan a first step today.

To Journal

What one thing was most hurtful when you were growing up? What was lacking? What kind of family do you wish you had? What kind of family would you/do you want to create?

Prayer

Dear Jesus, true communion with others is hard in this life, even with those who are closest. Sometimes life together seems impossible. But I know nothing is impossible with You.

May 12

I am everything for you. Don't place that burden on anyone else—it's not fair.

God's word

"For in him all the fullness of God was pleased to dwell . . ." (Colossians 1:19). "And you have come to fullness of life in him . . ." (Colossians 2:10).

Words of Wisdom

Take advantage of the reality of your heavenly family: God is your good Father, Mary is your good Mother, and the saints are your older brothers and sisters. Make friends with them. Find church friends, too.

To do

Find ways to feel close to God. (He's already close to you!) When you feel alone, you are not really alone, so talk to Him. Relish times when you're not with others as deeper God-times. Open up to Him. Chatter away to Him!

To journal

Have you expected others to be God for you? (This is a common mistake for those dating and for married couples.) Have others expected you to be God for them? How can you deal with this?

Prayer

Dear Jesus, You are my Friend of friends. I'm sorry for ignoring You when I'm alone. Help me take advantage of these times as *our* time.

May 13

I stand for families. I stand for individuals. I am on everyone's side.

God's Word

". . . I am their inheritance . . ." (Ezekiel 44:28). "Thou art a hiding place for me . . ." (Psalm 32:7). "For my father and mother have forsaken me, but the LORD will take me up" (Psalm 27:10).

Words of wisdom

Ancient cultures did not have the concept of the individual. Although families and groups are very important, never forget that we are all part of the larger community of the human family and the Church. In today's society, families and groups are breaking down. Many find themselves alone, whether or not they want to be.

To do

Are you solicitous of those who have no family: orphans, the elderly, immigrants, the homeless, outcasts? What can you do to be someone else's family?

To journal

In life we need a balance between the individual's needs and aspirations, and those of the family or community. God relates to us individually as well as in a group. Comment on your own experience of this tension.

Prayer

Dear Jesus, my deepest identity is in You.

May 14

I do not want slaves. I want friends and family members.

God's Word

". . . [H]e chose us in him before the foundation of the world. . . .
He destined us in love to be his sons through Jesus Christ . . ."
(Ephesians 1:4–5).

Words of Wisdom

You can't choose your family, but you can choose your friends.
Sometimes family members are our best friends, sometimes a friend
is closer than a brother. Friendships are essential—even just for our
bodies to stay healthy! Older people often die quickly after their
spouse dies, or die years before their time if they live alone. If you
can't prove you have a support system—family and friends to help
you recover—you won't even be considered for receiving an organ
donation. If newborn babies aren't picked up and held they may
die.

To Do

Consider today what role respectful and appropriate hugging
and touching has in your friendships. Do you pull away? Do you
reach out to others?

To Journal

Write about a time when family or friends were your lifesavers.

Prayer

Dear Jesus, help me to understand and live my dignity not only
as a child of God, but also as Your friend.

May 15

Be a good friend. By being a good friend you will attract good friends. If you have found even one true, good friend in your life, you have found a treasure beyond counting.

God's Word

"A friend loves at all times . . ." (Proverbs 17:17).

Words of Wisdom

Friendship is a great school of love and intimacy. The word "intimacy" has come to be associated only with sex, but there are many ways that we can and must be intimate with others! Intimacy means knowing and being known, revealing ourselves to others we trust, and letting them reveal themselves to us.

To do

Be there when your friends need you. Be willing to give in and not have your way. Don't talk about yourself all the time. Be genuinely interested in others. Be a good listener.

To journal

What areas do you need to grow in to be a better friend, to grow in intimacy? What areas are you strong in?

Prayer

Dear Jesus, you never let Your friends down, but loved them to the end despite their denial, betrayal, cowardice, and confusion. Help me to be a dependable friend.

May 16

Being a good friend does not mean being a doormat. I was not a doormat. I was a friend who spoke and did the truth at all times.

God's word

". . . [F]or this I have come into the world, to bear witness to the truth" (John 18:37).

Words of wisdom

If a "friend" is constantly selfish or abusive, they're not a friend. Some people are not capable of intimate relationships because of psychological or emotional disorders, or because of the kind of person they've chosen to be. We need to break off unhealthy relationships that sap our ability to have other friends.

To do

Friends may speak hard truths to us about ourselves, but friends should spend most of their time encouraging us and building us up. Examine your friendships.

To journal

Loyalty does not mean "my friend, right or wrong," but helping my friend to be the best person possible, and always doing what's truly right for the friend and for myself, no matter the cost. Write about an experience you've had of loyalty.

Prayer

Dear Jesus, give me the ability and strength to create happy, healthy, and holy friendships, and remedy "friendships" that don't really exist.

May 17

Love everyone, but befriend people slowly.

God's Word

". . . I send you out as lambs in the midst of wolves" (Luke 10:3). "One who trusts others too quickly is light-minded . . ." (Sirach 19:4).

Words of Wisdom

Ralph Waldo Emerson's "Self-Reliance," the Horatio Algiers story, and Ayn Rand's doctrine of selfishness have influenced many. But we are called to be, and actually are, interdependent. However, we have to be prudent and cautious in our dealings with others, because not everyone has good will.

To do

What about helping others in Christian charity? That's fine, but if you are not trained in psychology or spiritual direction, you will not be able to help certain people who have been called "emotional vampires." They will end up thoroughly depleting you. Tell these people in your life where they can get help and distance yourself from these relationships.

To journal

Why did Jesus once tell His apostles to "greet no one on the road" (Luke 10:4)? Wasn't that "unChristian"? What might Jesus have been trying to teach the apostles?

Prayer

Help me befriend myself so that when I do make a gift of myself, it won't be compulsive, but a free gift, like Your gift of Yourself.

May 18

Are you a good friend to yourself? This is one of My commandments.

God's Word

"You shall love the Lord your God. . . .You shall love your neighbour as yourself" (Matthew 22:37, 39).

Words of wisdom

"Be your own best friend." "Make yourself good company." If we learn to do this, we'll know how to be a good friend to others. When you feel yourself getting into a negative thought spiral, recite Scripture passages that speak of God's love and promises to you.

To do

Women in particular have a problem with not loving ourselves enough because we are frequently reaching out to love and nurture others. Many pressures and expectations are placed on women. *Loving Yourself More: 101 Meditations on Self-Esteem for Women*, by Virginia Froehle, can help.

To journal

Write about how you love yourself and fail to love yourself.

Prayer

Dear Jesus, I can never love myself as much as You love me. I can never outdo You in love. I am called to love infinitely as You do, and that includes loving myself.

May 19

Are you developing your relationship with yourself? I created you, but you are co-creating yourself daily by your words and actions.

God's Word

"But the souls of the righteous are in the hand of God, and no torment will ever touch them" (Wisdom 3:1).

Words of Wisdom

Babies grow toward consciousness: self-consciousness, full consciousness, consciousness of God. It never stops—through to eternity! We should always be awakening more and more to God and the life of the Spirit.

To do

Watch the movie *Wide Awake*. What does the little boy in the movie become "wide awake" to?

To journal

Consciousness and conscience go hand in hand. Consciousness is awareness. Conscience is the faculty that helps us make choices out of our awareness. We need God and the Church to guide both, because we are creatures who need to live in accord with the natural and divine order.

Prayer

Dear Jesus, You are described as the "only necessary Being." You are Being itself. I glory in my dependence on You.

May 20

Love people. Don't shut your heart to anyone. People are My best creation.

"He who does not love abides in death" (1 John 3:14).

"It doesn't cost two cents to smile and be kind." Some people are naturally gregarious, but all of us are called to widen our circle of friends, to have an interesting array of acquaintances that aren't all the same.

Not everyone I know is my bosom buddy, but neither is anyone a distant stranger. List acquaintances and friends. Am I spending too much time with acquaintances and not enough time with true friends? How about online?

Is it possible to have too many friends? Yes—if I've made them all think they're close friends, and I can't keep up with them all. Is it possible to have too few friends? Yes—if I keep to myself too much. Am I too friendly? Too aloof? What can I do so that people don't feel either too close or too neglected by me?

Dear Jesus, help me strike the proper balance of friendliness with everyone according to the priority they hold in my life.

May 21

*Do you like the way I've made you on the inside? It's on the inside—
with My grace—that you can make the biggest changes.*

God's word

"In a large house there are utensils not only of gold and silver but
also of wood and clay, some for special use, some for ordinary" (2
Timothy 2:20 NRSV).

Words of wisdom

Some people are naturally extroverted: outgoing, energized by
being around people. Some people are naturally introverted: inward,
energized by time alone. Which are you? We can't change our basic
temperament (and shouldn't want to), but we can grow in the opposite tendency.

To do

Shyness is not introversion, it's anxiety. Are you shy or know
someone who is? Learn ways to help overcome shyness for yourself
or others.

To journal

Are you more geared to action or reflection? How about your
friends and family members? How can you be more understanding
toward them, knowing their basic disposition?

Prayer

Dear Jesus, please help people who are shy because they fear
some possible humiliation. Sometimes this is me. Help me take the
focus off myself.

May 22

I did not create you to be alone. Find friends, create friends. Find community, create community.

God's Word

". . . [T]he LORD . . . who formed the earth and made it . . . formed it to be inhabited!" (Isaiah 45:18) ". . . [I]f we love one another, God abides in us and his love is perfected in us" (1 John 4:12).

Words of Wisdom

Even if circumstances of health, studies, work, or location mean you are frequently alone, find a way to balance that with "people" time. Nobody really wants to be alone all the time, nor is it good for us!

To do

If you're not used to initiating friendships and community, if you find it awkward and challenging, remember that people are amazing, especially "church people." Join something at church and you'll find new friends.

To journal

Rephrase the words of the Simon and Garfunkel song "I Am a Rock" according to the reality of our interdependence (e.g., "I Am a Jigsaw Puzzle Piece").

Prayer

Dear Jesus, when people feel completely unconnected, terrible things happen to them, and sometimes to those in their path. Let there always be a friend for everyone, and let me do my part.

May 23

Friendship is one of those things in life that really matters, that really lasts, even into eternity.

God's Word

". . . [T]he soul of Jonathan was knit to the soul of David, and Jonathan loved him as his own soul" (1 Samuel 18:1). ". . . [Y]our people shall be my people, and your God my God . . ." (Ruth 1:16).

Words of Wisdom

Those who work with Alzheimer's patients have discovered that the word "friend" still has great meaning for their patients. To win an Alzheimer's patient's trust, introduce yourself by saying: "I'm your friend."

To do

Write an old-fashioned, long-hand, snail-mail letter to those you will still want as friends in fifty years. What are some famous friendships in history? How can you purposefully strengthen your friendships to last? Read *Born for Friendship* by Bernard Basset, or the classic, *Spiritual Friendship* by Aelred of Rievaulx.

To journal

Write about your various friendships growing up. How have they changed, grown weaker, or grown stronger?

Prayer

Dear Jesus, thank You for the gift of friendship. Send me new friends if I need them, help me enrich the friendships I have. Enlarge my capacity for true friendship.

May 24

Your friendships in this world prepare you for the communion of heaven. They are worth your time and effort!

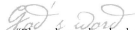

God's word

"Blessed are the dead who die in the Lord . . ." (Revelation 14:13).

Words of Wisdom

We can't go at life alone. Even physically, we are an immense, interlocking, interacting network of organisms, totally interdependent on each other for everything. In the spiritual order, everything we do affects everyone else, for good and bad. Some of our best friends can be saints who've gone before us to heaven, and are cheering us on.

To do

Learn about saints and holy people who lived closest to our times: *Big Book of Women Saints* by Sarah Gallick, *Literary Converts* by Joseph Pearce, *John Paul II's Book of Saints* by Matthew Bunson, *Faces of Holiness* by Ann Ball, *Saints of the Americas* by Arturo Perez-Rodriguez.

To journal

Who are your favorite saints? Why? What is your friendship with each one like? Do you have a Confirmation saint? Why did you choose them?

Prayer

Dear Jesus, I don't ever need to feel lonely, but when loneliness does creep in, it's ultimately a longing for heaven, isn't it?

May 25

Talking isn't automatically communicating, but it's a start. Communicating isn't automatically community, but it's a start. Community isn't automatically communion, but it's a start.

God's Word

"Put out into the deep . . ." (Luke 5:4).

Words of Wisdom

The younger generation is the most plugged-in, wired, media-savvy, keeping-in-touch generation ever. Yet as one young person said: "We still get insecure, lonely and depressed." Why? We're all human, of course. Could it also be a need to *deepen* all that communication, or make more of it face-to-face?

To Do

If we continually block out others through our use of personal, individualized media, we create more loneliness in the world. Talk to friends and family about media use and communicate better with them. Agree to make the table a media-tech-free zone!

To Journal

What is your experience with all the latest media technologies? Do you make media work for you so that they enhance your life with others? How? How do you balance giving your undivided attention to those in front of you and communicating through technology?

Prayer

Dear Jesus, You desire that communications technologies bring us together, not isolate us or drive wedges between us. Help me use media technology responsibly and lovingly.

May 26

My Holy Spirit brings the world together and creates communion. Open your life to Him.

God's word

"Have you heard a word [gossip]? Let it die with you. Be brave! It will not make you burst!" (Sirach 19:10)

Words of wisdom

Deepen *what* you talk about beyond games, sports, clothes, hair, shopping, and who's dating who. Is there a need to humanize *how* communication is done by slowing it down, using complete sentences, listening more, not *always* having earbuds in your ears, giving the gift of your unwired bodily presence to others?

To do

Read *Media Mindfulness* by Gretchen Hailer and Rose Pacatte, or *Infinite Bandwidth* by Eugene Gan, books with practical ideas of how to use media intentionally. Read John Paul II's small document on new media, *Rapid Development*.

To journal

God is everywhere, including our wired, often virtual world. How can you be attentive to God *through* media? How and where do you already find God in our mediated world?

Prayer

Dear Jesus, Pope Benedict said these scary words, "We are no longer able to hear God—there are too many different frequencies filling our ears." Please don't let that be me.

May 27

Where is your community? I save you as an individual, but also as part of a community. Where do you seek communion?

God's Word

".... [Y]ou may ... become partakers of the divine nature" (2 Peter 1:4).

Words of wisdom

One of Pope Benedict's favorite words is "communion." He used it ten times in a short talk on a World Day of Prayer for Vocations. Communication should lead to community, which should lead to communion. Keep trying. Don't look at results. We don't get to quit.

To do

"Holy Communion" means just that—beautiful union with Jesus. When we can't get to daily Mass, and actually any time we want, we can make "spiritual Communions," asking Jesus to come into us as if we had received Holy Communion.

To journal

When do you feel you're least in communion with God and others? When are you most aware of your communion with others and with God?

Prayer

Dear Jesus, You are perfect *communication,* the Word of God. Your Church is perfect *community* because we live in You. Heaven is perfect *communion* because we will share as fully as we can in the intimacy of the Trinity. I can't wait.

May 28

Do you know where you came from? From Me. But your existence is the culmination of a long chain of history!

God's Word

"Let this be recorded for a generation to come, so that a people yet unborn may praise the LORD . . ." (Psalm 102:18).

Words of Wisdom

It is commonly said that whoever doesn't know history is bound to repeat it. Get to know your roots: your family history, ethnic history, and world history, but most of all get to know your spiritual history by reading and studying salvation history: the Bible and Church history.

To Do

Read the Acts of the Apostles and watch *A.D.* or *Peter and Paul*. Read Church history like *A Compact History of the Catholic Church* by Alan Schreck. Get a good Bible commentary to help you verse by verse as you read the Bible like *The New Jerome Biblical Commentary* or *Collegeville Bible Commentary*.

To Journal

How would you describe your little place in the universe? Read Max Erhmann's famous poem, "Desiderata" for inspiration.

Prayer

Dear Jesus, no one is an outsider, unplanned, or an accident. Each of us was loved by You from all eternity. I rejoice in my little place in Your creation and kingdom!

May 29

Do you obey My Church? The Church is My gift to you as your sure path to heaven.

God's Word

". . . [T]he church of the living God, the pillar and bulwark of the truth" (1 Timothy 3:15).

Words of Wisdom

"Jesus did not leave us orphans. He gave us the gift of the Church, born from His open side on the cross, to help guide us and keep us on the right track. Let us be grateful for this gift and pray especially for our Holy Father." (Sr. M. Agnes Labbé, FSGM, www.altonfranciscans.org)

To Do

Investigate St. John Bosco's vision of the Church as a boat. What saved the boat? Read more about the Catholic Church in the *Catechism of the Catholic Church* (nos. 748–975).

To Journal

The Church is often called the "barque" or "boat of Peter." Write about your favorite image of the Church: Society, Mystical Body of Christ, Sacrament, Mother, Pilgrim People, Servant, Bride of Christ, Communion of Saints, or something else. Why is it your favorite?

Prayer

Dear Jesus, thank You for our holy Mother, the Church, where I am home.

May 30

I have the whole world in My hands. Do you have the whole world in your heart?

God's word

"Go therefore and make disciples of all nations, baptizing them in the name of the Father and of the Son and of the Holy Spirit" (Matthew 28:19).

Words of wisdom

If you aren't going to be a missionary to other lands, be sure to pray for missionaries and have a missionary heart that is concerned for and learns about the needs of the world. Also, the traditionally Christian parts of the world are in great need of re-evangelization. You can be a missionary in your own backyard!

To do

"Adopt" a missionary. Pray for them. Start a correspondence with them. Find out what they need and raise money or collect goods.

To journal

Write out your witness of what God has done for you, how He makes a difference in your life, what your life was like without God (if you've had that experience). Tell your story, no matter how small, for much holiness is lost from people not telling their stories.

Prayer

Dear Jesus, people have a right to know You. Let me be Your messenger. Send me!

May 31

Where the Church suffers and is persecuted, it grows. Pray for your persecuted brothers and sisters. Support them.

God's word

". . . I saw under the altar the souls of those who had been slain for the word of God and for the witness they had borne . . ." (Revelation 6:9).

Words of wisdom

"The blood of the martyrs is the seed of the faith" (Tertullian). Learn about parts of the world where there is no religious freedom or the Church is persecuted.

To do

Read about the martyrs in *The North American Martyrs* by Lillian Fisher, *Bl. Miguel Pro* by Ann Ball, *Here I Am, Lord* by Jeanne Evans and Ita Ford, and *In Solitary Witness* by Gordon Zahn.

To journal

Can you see yourself as a missionary or a martyr? Martyr simply means witness (and the most powerful witness is to give one's life). In your own country, is the Church appreciated? Resented? Tolerated? Harassed? What can you do to help it stand firm?

Prayer

Dear Jesus, I have "not yet resisted to the point of shedding blood" (cf. Hebrews 12:4). May I witness always to Your goodness by a daily martyrdom, bloodless or not, so that others may believe and share Your joy.

June 1

You are part of an amazing story, an amazing drama, an amazing mystery. Will you enter fully into the story, the drama, the mystery?

God's word

"I came that they may have life, and have it abundantly" (John 10:10 NRSV). "No one has ever seen God; the only Son, who is in the bosom of the Father, he has made him known" (John 1:18).

Words of wisdom

What is the "Christian mystery"? It's the Trinity: Father, Son, and Holy Spirit. The Trinity is eternal love given and received, but the Trinity is not closed in on itself. The Trinity has opened up to us in Jesus's life, death, and resurrection!

To do

The Mass is the *celebration* of the Christian mystery. The next time you're at Mass, tell yourself: "This is how I participate in the divine life of the Trinity." Eucharist is where we participate in God's gift to us. By giving and receiving we are participating in the exchange of God's divine love.

To journal

We tell a story to find a story. What does this mean?

Prayer

Dear Jesus, I don't need to create my own drama, do I? I am already a part of the greatest drama.

June 2

Come to My altar, come to My table, where I will give you My very self.

God's Word

"Go out to the highways . . . and compel people to come in, that my house may be filled" (Luke 14:23).

Words of Wisdom

All are invited to God's heavenly banquet and liturgy which begins here on earth in the Eucharistic Liturgy. When you invite others to God's table, you are acting as God's party planner! Liturgy means the participation of the people of God in the work of God. It is also an action of the Church, making the Church present as a sign of the communion between God and man.

To Do

Make a poster or fancy invitation to remind yourself of what the Mass really is: "Jesus of Nazareth, Master of the Universe, invites you to a dinner in His honor. Please bring with you the poor and lowly, and a heart full of love." Send invitations to friends!

To Journal

How is liturgy the source of your life?

Prayer

Dear Jesus, my whole life is supposed to be a liturgy. Nothing is too small, insignificant or mundane to be part of the liturgy of my life offered to You.

June 3

All your prayer finds its source and goal in My prayer, My sacrifice, My feast.

God's Word

"And Melchizedek king of Salem brought out bread and wine; he was priest of God Most High" (Genesis 14:18). "On this mountain the LORD of hosts will make for all peoples a feast . . ." (Isaiah 25:6). "This is my blood of the covenant, which is poured out for many" (Mark 14:24).

Words of wisdom

The Mass is primarily where we grow in faith and are transformed by Jesus. In the Mass we share in Christ as priests (worship), prophets (proclamation of the Word), and kings (service). The whole life of the Church flows from the Eucharist.

To do

Read the *Catechism of the Catholic Church*, Part Two, which is all about the meaning of worship and the sacraments in our lives. Read Vatican II's *Dogmatic Constitution on the Sacred Liturgy*.

To journal

What does salvation mean to you? How does it make you feel when you see those "Jesus Saves" signs?

Prayer

Dear Jesus, the Mass is the Last Supper, the Crucifixion, the Resurrection all in one. Open my eyes to all that the Mass is!

June 4

I communicate the gifts and fruits of My redemption to you in very concrete ways that you can touch, taste, smell, see, and hear.

God's word

"... God ... has blessed us in Christ with every spiritual blessing ..." (Ephesians 1:3). "O LORD, how manifold are your works! In wisdom you have made them all; the earth is full of your creatures" (Psalm 104:24 NRSV).

Words of wisdom

All God does is bless us. His action toward us is never, ever tainted with any kind of malice. Humankind, in choosing to move away from God, chooses death over and over, but God is always blessing us to direct us back to life. In the liturgy, the fullness of God's blessings for salvation in history is revealed.

To do

Listen to the song "All Good Gifts" from the musical *Godspell*. (The lyrics are the original words from the *Episcopal Hymnal* by Matthias Claudius, 1782.)

To journal

Copy down: "The day we cease to burn with the divine fire of God, souls will die of the cold" (Paul Claudel, poet and former atheist).

Prayer

Dear Jesus, I am in great need of You. Don't let me retreat from Your fire for any reason.

June 5

Through my offering, once and for all, I continuously renew the whole world.

God's word

"From the rising of the sun to its setting the name of the LORD is to be praised!" (Psalm 113:3)

Words of wisdom

The Mass is the work/action of the whole Trinity. The Father blesses us and we bless him back in return. The Son is present in the Eucharist, the Church, the priest, the word. The Holy Spirit—the "living memory of the Church"—opens our hearts to the spiritual understanding of the Scriptures and makes present past events of our salvation.

To do

Open your heart and pray for the whole world at every Mass you participate in. (You can also offer up all the Masses said each day everywhere in the world without attending them!)

To journal

The Holy Spirit transforms our lives during the Mass and creates communion among human beings, breaking down all barriers. When have you experienced this at Mass?

Prayer

Dear Jesus, Your Holy Spirit transforms the water and wine into Your Body and Blood, as He overshadowed Mary at your conception. Let me be that open to receive what You have for me.

June 6

The Old Covenant contained the foundations and promise of My New Covenant. It is a seamless continuum.

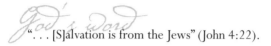

God's Word

". . . [S]alvation is from the Jews" (John 4:22).

Words of Wisdom

Old Testament events retain their original significance, but now have added meaning: they find their fulfillment in Christ. For example, the flood prefigured Baptism, and manna prefigured the Eucharist. The more we familiarize ourselves with ancient and contemporary Jewish liturgy, the more we'll discover the depth and riches of our Christian liturgy!

To do

Remember that Jesus, Mary, Joseph, the Apostles, and the first Christians were Jews. Pope Pius XII once said, "Spiritually, we are all Semites." Take a tour of a synagogue and see how many similarities you find to our Catholic faith and liturgy!

To journal

Christians are sometimes mystified that not all Jews accepted Jesus while He was on earth. Read Paul's Letter to the Romans, chapters 9–11, then write out your understanding of God's faithfulness toward and plan for His Chosen People.

Prayer

Dear Jesus, help me learn about and appreciate my Jewish heritage!

June 7

The earthly liturgy is a reflection of the heavenly liturgy. Heaven is My liturgy and My wedding feast at the same time. You're invited, and best of all, you're the bride!

God's Word

"If then you have been raised with Christ, seek the things that are above, where Christ is, seated at the right hand of God" (Colossians 3:1).

Words of Wisdom

The "whole Christ" celebrates the liturgy, that is, Christ the head, and Christ the body, on earth and in heaven. God's angels are also present at every liturgy! No liturgy is private, but a celebration of the whole Church—which calls and draws all of humanity into communion.

To Do

Sing "We Are One Body," by Dana, at the top of your lungs.

To Journal

Vatican II stressed "full, conscious, and active participation" in the liturgy (*Dogmatic Constitution on the Sacred Liturgy*, no. 14). This does not necessarily mean being a lector or extraordinary Eucharistic minister. It can be done from your pew. How?

Prayer

Dear Jesus, we are all a "chosen race, a royal priesthood, a holy nation" (1 Peter 2:9). Help me live my Baptism and my "priesthood of the faithful!"

June 8

I am the one, true High Priest. Your ordained priests share in My ministry and are icons of Me.

God's word
". . . [T]hat he might become a merciful and faithful high priest in the service of God, to make expiation for the sins of the people" (Hebrews 2:17).

Words of Wisdom
The Mass is not different sacrifices offered every day, but the same sacrifice of Jesus, present again. At Mass, eternity enters time. We don't go back in time, but Christ's saving action is made present in the here and now!

To do
Get a depiction of Jesus on the cross dressed in liturgical vestments (usually called "Christ the High Priest") to remind you what the cross and the Mass really are. Pray for vocations to the priesthood! Pray for your priests!

To journal
What does the Mass mean to you? How can you grow in your understanding and love of the Mass? How have you been helped and changed through the ministry of priests? (Why not tell them?)

Prayer
"You are worthy of everything, every word of praise, every song we will ever sing, / fountain of all grace. / Our High Priest! / Make us a house of peace."

June 9

The entire cosmos speaks of Me, reveals My love, My patterns, and My plans for you! The cosmos is personal! Take it personally! My cosmic designs are now incorporated in the liturgy.

God's Word

"For from the greatness and beauty of created things comes a corresponding perception of their Creator" (Wisdom 13:5).

Words of Wisdom

Signs, symbols, and social gestures were incorporated into the Old Covenant and took on special significance (anointing, washing, sacrifice, etc.). Jesus Christ used signs, symbols, and gestures (healing, parables, the Passover, etc.) and gave them their ultimate meaning: Himself!

To do

The Eucharist is *the* sacrament, par excellence. The Church itself is a sacrament. Look up and memorize the definition of sacrament.

To journal

Which tangible symbols from nature (light, water, wind, fire, etc.) or from social life (washing feet, breaking bread, giving gifts, etc.) that are part of liturgical celebrations most touch you? Why? Why do you think filmmakers have a great appreciation of the Church's "sacramental system"?

Prayer

Dear Jesus, You are there through Your Church at all the important times in our lives: when we're "hatched, matched, and dispatched." Thank You for accompanying us on our pilgrimage back to You!

June 10

I promised I would not abandon you. There are reminders of Me everywhere, even in the arts you yourselves have crafted.

God's word

". . . [T]he Word was God" (John 1:1). "He is the image of the invisible God . . ." (Colossians 1:15).

Words of wisdom

Jesus is both the Word and image of the Father. Sacred music and sacred art enrich liturgy, and illumine and interpret one another. In the Eastern Church, only the human voice is used (not musical instruments), and sacred icons are used in procession during the liturgy.

To do

Make sure you have an outlet to be creative, and take time to create! Try music, art, writing, designing, cooking, teaching, science, fixing things, yoga, dancing, sports, caring for people and animals, or gardening. How do *you* prefer to create?

To journal

Journal about a piece of sacred art that is imprinted on your memory. Journal about a hymn, sacred music, or sacred film. What do you find striking that moves you to worship?

Prayer

Dear Jesus, we long to see You, and You have surrounded us with Yourself, even through the creations of our minds and hearts and hands. Thank You for Your abundant, abiding presence.

June 11

You are an artist whether you know it or not, because I am an artist and you are My image.

God's word

"Men who will not acknowledge the coming of Jesus Christ in the flesh; such a one is the deceiver and the antichrist" (2 John 1:7).

Words of wisdom

God forbade His people to make images because they might worship them. (However, even in Old Testament times, God commanded several images to be made under His supervision: the seraph serpent, angels on the ark of the covenant, etc.)

To do

Get a book of icons that explains their symbolism. Visit an Eastern Rite or Orthodox church and ask for an explanation of their icons. Visit an art museum and look for "sacred" art.

To journal

Do you rejoice when you see an image of Our Lord, Our Lady, or the angels and saints? They are meant to make us feel happy, like when we look at photos of our friends and family. Describe (or sketch!) your favorite image of Jesus or Mary in a church near you.

Prayer

Dear Jesus, please continue to inspire contemporary artists to depict You in contemporary ways to inspire contemporary people!

June 12

I lead you through time: each year, each month, each day. Enter into all My Church's liturgical seasons, celebrations, and feasts.

God's word

"He gave beauty to the feasts, and arranged their times throughout the year, while they praised God's holy name, and the sanctuary resounded from early morning" (Sirach 47:10).

Words of wisdom

The liturgical year relives the life of Christ from His Incarnation to the anticipation of His Second Coming. Bl. James Alberione described the liturgical year as going up a mountain by spiraling around it. Every year we end up in the same place . . . except we're a little higher!

To do

Do you feel the need for Bible study or more Bible reading? Read the Bible with the Church! Use the daily liturgical Scriptures for your Bible reading. The whole Church all over the world will be reading the same Scriptures with you.

To journal

What's your favorite liturgical season? Why? What are some ways you can better celebrate the liturgical seasons? How do you celebrate Ordinary Time?

Prayer

Dear Jesus, I don't need to starve! Help me nourish and sanctify myself at the Church's feast of the liturgical year.

June 13

On Sunday, enter into My rest. Learn to put earthly cares aside for one day of the week. Learn the meaning of the word rejoice!

God's Word

". . . [T]his day is holy to our LORD; and do not be grieved, for the joy of the LORD is your strength" (Nehemiah 8:10).

Words of Wisdom

Sunday is the seventh day, the day of the sun, the Lord's Day, on which God rested from creation. It is the day of Christ's Resurrection, the first day of the week. It is also the "new day," the "day that the Lord has made," "the day that knows no evening" (cf. Psalm 118:24). What is there *not* to celebrate?

To do

Reflect on Seurat's *A Sunday on La Grande Jatte*. What does this painting tell you about Sunday?

To journal

Write about your childhood experiences of Sunday. Were they special? Was there something you loved about them? Were they centered on the Lord's Supper? Now that you're in charge of your own Sundays, how will you make them special?

Prayer

Dear Jesus, every Sunday is a little Easter, the feast of feasts, the solemnity of solemnities. Teach me to partake fully of Your festivities!

June 14

You are part of My beautiful, rich garden of humanity. Do you know who you are? Do you know your own particular beauty?

God's Word

"She was beautiful in appearance, and had a very lovely face. . . . No one spoke ill of her, for she feared God with great devotion" (Judith 8:7–8).

Words of Wisdom

One of the major differences between the (Western) Latin Rite and the Eastern Rite is that the East uses lots of color, art, candles, incense, whereas the West—in the austere but rich Roman tradition—is no-frills and minimalistic, even in the language of its prayers. What is the beauty of each approach?

To Do

Learn about your personal Catholic heritage. What nationality(ies) are you? What are some specific Catholic customs of these countries? Music? Prayers? How can you celebrate these?

To Journal

Differences are a call to communion, not necessarily conformity, and certainly not antagonism! How have you felt the differences of others calling you to communion?

Prayer

Dear Jesus, You are King of the Nations. Open my mind and heart more and more to all the amazing human cultures and liturgies of the world!

June 15

I call all My children to new life in Baptism.

God's Word

"Therefore, if any one is in Christ, he is a new creation . . ." (2 Corinthians 5:17).

Words of Wisdom

Baptism, Confirmation, and Eucharist are "Sacraments of Initiation," introducing us into the body of Christ. Baptism and Confirmation cannot be repeated, whereas we can receive the Eucharist many times throughout our lives. Baptism is our "all access" pass to all the good things God wants to give us! Baptism removes original sin; gives us sanctifying grace (the divine life of God in us); makes us heirs of heaven; infuses faith, hope, and love; makes us able to receive the other sacraments; makes us members of the Church.

To do

Read Nicodemus's conversation with Jesus about Baptism (John 3:1–21).

To journal

There's a song entitled "I Was Born to Worship the Lord," by Lenny LeBlanc, that answers a very fundamental question. What else do you feel you were born to do?

Prayer

Dear Jesus, I reject Satan and all his empty promises. I reject the glamour of evil and refuse to be mastered by sin. I want to live in the glorious light of Your children!

June 16

Baptism is My free gift, not a mental exercise. That is why babies come to My font. I give them grace, I incorporate them into Myself.

God's word

"Let the children come to me, do not hinder them; for to such belongs the kingdom of God" (Mark 10:14).

Words of wisdom

Bl. James Alberione said, "Make people children of God; this is everything." Everyone is a child of God in the sense that God is the Creator, but God wants to share His divine life with everyone, and wants everyone to be a part of His Mystical Body, the Church, through Baptism.

To do

Memorize the wonderful effects of Baptism (see June 15th).

To journal

Parents choose good things for their children all the time, even things the child might not choose for themselves (think math and peas). What could be a better choice than Baptism? When we're old enough, we must make faith our own. How have you claimed your Baptism? How are you living a "sacramental life"?

Prayer

Dear Jesus, before I even knew You, You claimed me as Your own. Now I claim You as my own forever!

June 17

You are the temple of My Holy Spirit. In Confirmation, you experience the laying on of hands; you are anointed and sent forth. Confirmation is your Pentecost!

God's word

"Repent, and be baptized every one of you in the name of Jesus Christ . . . and you shall receive the gift of the Holy Spirit" (Acts 2:38).

Words of wisdom

Confirmation completes your Baptism with the seal of the Holy Spirit. Haven't been confirmed yet? Delay no longer! God wants to finish what He started! It will be a great source of grace, and will embolden you to live and share your faith.

To do

Memorize: "Come, Holy Spirit, fill the hearts of Your faithful and enkindle in them the fire of Your love. Send forth Your Spirit, O Lord, and they shall be created; and You will renew the face of the earth."

To journal

Like Baptism, Confirmation does not need full mental comprehension in order to be effective. However, the sacraments lead to spiritual maturity. How would you describe your spiritual maturity?

Prayer

Dear Jesus, spiritual maturity is not based on physical maturity. Children can achieve spiritual maturity, while some adults haven't reached it yet. Help me grow to Your "full stature".

June 18

Anointing has always been an important symbol. Oil is a sign of abundance, joy, cleansing, athleticism, healing, beauty, and strength. It marks you as belonging to Me. Do you want the whole universe to know you are Mine?

God's Word

"[O]n him has God the Father set his seal" (John 6:27).

Words of Wisdom

Confirmation means that baptismal grace is both confirmed and strengthened. Baptism, Confirmation, and Holy Orders confer an indelible spiritual mark or "character" on the soul that marks us as witnesses of Jesus Christ.

To do

What do you feel you have been anointed to do? Read the section on Confirmation in the *Catechism of the Catholic Church* (nos. 1285–1321). How does the celebration of Confirmation differ in the Eastern Church and the (Western) Latin Church? What is each Church trying to emphasize by the different ways they celebrate Confirmation?

To journal

Christ means "anointed one," and therefore, so does Christian. How does the fact that you are anointed in Baptism, and then again at Confirmation change how you think of yourself?

Prayer

Dear Jesus, how great is my dignity! You "lift up the lowly to a place with the princes of your people" (cf. Psalms 113:7–8).

June 19

I long for you far more than you long for Me! Don't stay away. Come to Me, receive Me in the Eucharist as often as you can. I will purify you, heal you, love you, strengthen you, enkindle you.

God's Word

". . . I am with you always, to the close of the age" (Matthew 28:20).

Words of Wisdom

All Eucharistic adoration outside of Mass flows from the Mass and leads back to it. Remember that Eucharistic devotion is not one devotion among many, it is *the* devotion of our whole lives and the whole Church!

To Do

Learn about St. Pius X lowering the age of first Holy Communion and encouraging daily Communion. Read *Sacrament of Charity* by Pope Benedict XVI, and *Christ Lives in Me* by Bl. James Alberione.

To Journal

Write out these lines of *"Ave, Verum Corpus"*: "Lord, we contemplate You in love. Keep our hearts and eyes fixed on You until we see You face to face in glory."

Prayer

"O food of travelers. . . . O manna of the heavenly. . . . Do not deprive of sweetness the hearts of those who seek You. . . . Grant that, having removed the veil, we will see You in heaven, Face to face" (*"Adoro Te"*).

June 20

My love would not permit Me to leave you alone. I not only sent My Holy Spirit, but I devised a way to stay in your churches where we can visit with each other.

God's Word

". . . [S]omething greater than Jonah is here" (Matthew 12:41).

Words of Wisdom

Since a sacrament is defined as "an outward sign instituted by Christ to give grace," "a tangible expression of an intangible grace," "a real symbol that actually accomplishes what it signifies," then the Holy Eucharist, the Most Blessed Sacrament, is the Sacrament of Sacraments!

To Do

Participate in public Eucharistic devotion such as holy hours and Eucharistic processions. If none are available in your area, volunteer to help get them going.

To journal

Non-Catholic Christians have told Catholics: "If I believed what you say you believe about that piece of bread, I would crawl on my hands and knees to Communion." What are ways you show your love and reverence for Jesus in the Blessed Sacrament?

Prayer

Dear Jesus, I love You above all things, and I desire to receive You into my soul. Since I cannot at this moment receive You sacramentally, come at least spiritually into my heart.

June 21

I am your Divine Physician. I long to heal you. Come to Me. I will make you new over and over again.

God's Word

"Peace. . . . Receive the Holy Spirit" (John 20:21–22).

Words of Wisdom

The sacraments give us "sacramental grace," that is, grace that accomplishes precisely what the sacrament is supposed to accomplish. The Sacrament of Penance (or Reconciliation) can help us to avoid re-committing the specific sin(s) we are confessing!

To do

If possible, find a good confessor that you can go to at regular intervals. Sometimes a good confessor can be as helpful as a spiritual director (they can even be the same priest). Find a priest who understands that you want to use Confession as a sacrament of healing for venial sins and weaknesses also.

To journal

Bl. James Alberione used to speak of "Confession for progress," or "progressive Confession," that is, the use of Confession to make progress in overcoming our predominant sin. How have you found Confession progressive? What progress would you like to make in Confession?

Prayer

Dear Jesus, thank You for Your sacramental grace attached to the Sacrament of Penance which helps me with my most stubborn sins!

June 22

I want to take your stony heart and give you a natural heart, one that is turned in love toward Me and your brothers and sisters.

God's word

"Then I will teach transgressors your ways, and sinners will return to you" (Psalm 51:13 NRSV). "[I]f my people . . . humble themselves, and pray and seek my face, and turn from their wicked ways, then I will . . . forgive their sin and heal their land" (2 Chronicles 7:14).

Words of wisdom

We must live in continual conversion. Conversion simply means turning. We must constantly turn ourselves back to God, back to the narrow road.

To do

Prayer, fasting, and almsgiving are the three most important types of penance because they have to do with God, ourselves, and others. Acts of charity are the best penances of all. Start with acts of charity in thought and speech.

To journal

What kind of prayer, fasting, and almsgiving do you think the Lord wants from you? (Read Isaiah 58 to learn the kind of "fasting" the Lord desires.)

Prayer

"Restore us to yourself, O LORD, that we may be restored . . ." (Lamentations 5:21 NRSV).

June 23

I identify Myself with the sick and suffering. I suffer in you and with you. When you visit the sick, you are visiting Me.

God's Word

"Is any among you sick? Let him call for the elders of the church, and let them pray over him, anointing him with oil in the name of the Lord" (James 5:14).

Words of Wisdom

The Sacrament of the Anointing of the Sick is given to anyone in danger of death from sickness or old age, not just those at the moment of death. It is meant to bring healing or to help the person in their passage to eternal life.

To do

Visit someone you know who is chronically ill, disabled, elderly, or infirm. Ask him or her what good has come out of their ordeal.

To journal

Suffering can make us bitter or better. What has your experience of suffering been—in your own life or that of someone close to you?

Prayer

Dear Jesus, often illness and accidents are the only things to make us stop and think about the meaning of life, and return to You. I hope that I don't need that, but whatever it takes, Lord!

June 24

I desire to give you peace and courage at all times, but especially when you need it most, when you are facing trials.

God's word

"... I am the LORD, your healer" (Exodus 15:26).

Words of wisdom

God will grant physical healing if it is for the glory of God and the person's salvation. Every Mass is a "healing" Mass, and the Eucharist is linked with physical health (cf. John 6:54, 58; 1 Corinthians 11:30). Get used to asking God for all kinds of healings for yourself and others at every Mass!

To do

When we are weakened by suffering of whatever kind, we are more prone to discouragement, temptation, and despair. It is often next to impossible to pray. Create a regular program—if you don't already have one—of staying spiritually strong during the ordinary times of your life.

To journal

What has been your experience of God's physical or spiritual healing in your life or that of someone close to you?

Prayer

Dear Jesus, the most important kinds of healing are interior healing and healing from sin. I know that You will *always* grant this kind of healing. Let me not be focused only on physical healings.

June 25

My priests are on the front lines of the spiritual battle. They act in My name and person, but are still weak, sinful human beings. They need your prayers, friendship, encouragement, and support.

God's Word

"I tell you, Peter, the cock will not crow this day, until you three times deny that you know me" (Luke 22:34).

Words of Wisdom

Holy Orders (ministerial and ordained priesthood) and Matrimony are sacraments at the service of communion. In other words, they are sacraments of a particular vocation and mission.

To do

Think about sponsoring a priest in the missions. If you can't afford to sponsor a priest, why not "adopt" a priest and pray for him? Search online for "adopt a priest."

To journal

The Lord has given us a tremendous gift in His priests. Write to your favorite priest, thanking him. Write to the priests of your parish, assuring them of prayers. Write to a priest in the missions.

Prayer

Dear Jesus, "priests are sent by You, as You were sent by the Father. To them You have entrusted the treasures of Your doctrine, Your grace, and souls themselves. May they all be formed according to Your heart" (Prayers of the Pauline Family).

June 26

Bishops are the direct successors of My twelve apostles, and have the fullness of the sacrament of Holy Orders, that is, they have the office of sanctifying, teaching, and governing.

God's word

"Feed my sheep" (John 21:17).

Words of wisdom

All the baptized are the body of Christ, but the priest represents Christ as the head of the body. There are three degrees of the priesthood: bishops, priests, and deacons. The priesthood of the faithful is not a degree of the ministerial priesthood. It's a different kind of priesthood.

To do

Plan to go to the Chrism Mass at your cathedral on Holy Thursday, to join with the bishops and priests of your diocese. Learn about the history of your diocese, and the meaning of the motto and coat of arms of your bishop.

To journal

Write a letter to your bishop, assuring him of prayers. (A larger diocese will have an ordinary and perhaps auxiliary bishops to help him. Cardinals are special advisors to the Pope.)

Prayer

Dear Jesus, "may priests be the salt that purifies and preserves. In heaven, may they have around themselves, as a crown of joy, a multitude of souls!" (Prayers of the Pauline Family).

June 27

My people are irate about the heinous behavior of shepherds and pastors who preyed on the most innocent and defenseless in their flocks. I hear their cries.

God's word

"Woe to the world because of stumbling blocks! Occasions for stumbling are bound to come, but woe to the one by whom the stumbling block comes!" (Matthew 18:7 NRSV)

Words of wisdom

Horrific darkness was revealed in the Church. Casting light into the darkness will help eradicate it. We mustn't become cynical, believing the lie that this darkness is the true nature of the Church. Not all attacks on the Church are from the outside! How can an entity be more effectively toppled than from within?

To do

Who are some unsung heroic bishops and priests who never make the headlines for the good things they do? Be sure to publicize the good also.

To journal

How have you reacted to sexual abuse scandals involving bishops and priests? What do you believe is the solution to prevent future abuse?

Prayer

Dear Jesus, the Church is always in need of reform. It never seems to be free from corruption. Thank You for never leaving us, no matter how evil our deeds.

June 28

Marital love between a man and woman is an image of the love with which I love all humanity.

God's word

"For your Maker is your husband . . ." (Isaiah 54:5). ". . . '[T]he two shall become one flesh.' This mystery is a profound one, and I am saying that it refers to Christ and the church" (Ephesians 5:31–32).

Words of wisdom

Perhaps you haven't seen many good examples of faithful, unselfish married love. Although marriage—like all other aspects of human life—is plagued with sin, beautiful marriages are possible. The fault doesn't lie with marriage, it lies with sin! Couples can call on the grace of the sacrament of Matrimony to help them overcome the sin that tears them apart.

To do

Ask happily married couples what the "secrets" of their marriage and family life are. Compile their advice for yourself or friends who are getting married.

To journal

The purpose of marriage from the very beginning has been the bringing forth of new life and the good of the spouses. Describe how to create a holy, happy, healthy marriage for the long haul.

Prayer

Dear Jesus, help couples love one another with tender and fruitful love.

June 29

Don't be afraid of marriage. It isn't easy, but turn to Me and I will help you both. Marriage is a way of holiness! Make Me the center of your marriage.

God's Word

"Be subject to one another out of reverence for Christ" (Ephesians 5:21). "Bear one another's burdens . . ." (Galatians 6:2).

Words of Wisdom

Men and women are very different. Boyfriends and girlfriends, and husbands and wives need to talk together about what their various needs and expectations are (because they're different!), and explain their perspectives (because they're different!). Couples must pray together because their whole way of life is just that: to go to God together.

To do

Find comedic examples (sitcoms, books, movies, comic strips) that highlight the fact of just how different men and women are!

To journal

Copy down sentiments of true love found in the biblical books of Ruth, Tobit, and the Songs of Songs. This is God's plan for love—what love can be. What do you think is the difference between unrealistic romance and true romance?

Prayer

Dear Jesus, marriage is meant to make us more giving and less self-involved. Thank You for allowing marriage to save us from ourselves!

June 30

My Mother is the mother of all sacraments and sacramentals because it is she who first gave Me flesh and blood.

God's Word

"And God did extraordinary miracles by the hands of Paul, so that handkerchiefs or aprons were carried away from his body to the sick, and diseases left them and the evil spirits came out of them" (Acts 19:11–12).

Words of Wisdom

Sacramentals, or sacred signs, help us to receive the effects of the seven sacraments. Sacramentals are blessings and blessed objects such as medals, scapulars, and rosaries.

To Do

"There is hardly any proper use of material things which cannot thus be directed toward the sanctification of men and the praise of God." (*Dogmatic Constitution on the Sacred Liturgy,* no. 61)

What sacramentals do you use? Do you need to make more use of sacramentals?

To journal

The Church regulates sacramentals and other forms of "popular piety" to make sure they reflect sound doctrine. Have you witnessed an abuse of sacramentals that borders on superstition? What good uses of sacramentals have you witnessed?

Prayer

Dear Jesus, Catholicism is so earthy and touchy-feely! You have blessed us with every spiritual blessing!

July 1

My grace empowers you to imitate Me no matter what you struggle with.

God's Word

"[The LORD] loves the one who pursues righteousness" (Proverbs 15:9 NRSV). ". . . [M]ake every effort to supplement your faith with virtue . . ." (2 Peter 1:5).

Words of wisdom

Virtue is the habit of moral excellence. Virtue is doing the right thing—the true, good, beautiful, and loving thing—appropriate to every person and situation, no matter the cost. This comes from a heart filled with the love of Jesus.

To do

Identify which of the seven capital sins (pride, lust, envy, greed, sloth, anger, gluttony) you find yourself consistently most attracted to or falling into. What is the opposite virtue you need to practice? Pray and frequent the sacrament of Reconciliation in order to progress in this virtue.

To journal

Plan a strategy for practicing the virtue you need the most. Start with the small details. Examine your conscience daily and journal about failures and victories. Step up your effort as you make progress.

Prayer

Dear Jesus, I want to grow in the virtue I need most: _____. With You, all things are possible.

July 2

There are no shortcuts, quick fixes, or easy-ways-out in life. What fun would that be?

God's word

". . . [S]uffering produces endurance, and endurance produces character, and character produces hope" (Romans 5:3–4). "And above all these put on love . . ." (Colossians 3:14).

Words of wisdom

We need to make the practice of a particular virtue a habit in order for it to be fruitful (not just practice it sporadically). Bl. James Alberione said, "It is very, very, very difficult to do good." As soon as we step out in faith to do even a little bit of good, we will be opposed. "We are fighting not with flesh and blood, but with principalities and powers" (cf. Ephesians 6:12).

To do

If you practice one virtue, the rest will follow. It's almost impossible to practice just one virtue, because all the virtues are connected. Read *Virtue-Driven Life* by Fr. Groeschel, and *Seven Virtues* by Jean Donovan.

To journal

What is your experience of good habits and bad habits? Do they both "stick" the same?

Prayer

Dear Jesus, good *habits* sometimes make it easier to be good. However, help me to keep practicing virtue, whether it's easy or not.

July 3

Virtue does not lie at extremes, but in the middle where it often goes unnoticed.

God's word

"He has done all things well . . ." (Mark 7:37). ". . . [Y]our life is hid with Christ in God" (Colossians 3:3).

Words of wisdom

The middle does not mean being indecisive or equivocal. It means being balanced, which is a virtue in itself! Practicing virtue is like a gourmet meal with the right amount of every ingredient.

To do

Bravery lies in the middle of cowardice and foolhardiness. Generosity lies in the middle of stinginess and profligacy. Friendliness lies in the middle of stand-offishness and naïveté. Think of some more "radical middles" and their extremes.

To journal

Where have you gone overboard in either direction—lack or excess—in regard to various virtues, and wound up in vices (extremes)? The word "vice" comes from "viciousness." When society doesn't practice virtue, it becomes vicious. The word "virtue" comes from "vir" which means manliness (or womanliness!). When society practices virtue, it becomes humanized.

Prayer

Dear Jesus, often the extremes look like virtue. They're more exciting and showy. Help me to be where the action really is: in the radical middle.

July 4

I give you the light and grace you need to follow in My footsteps.

God's word

"And who is a rock, except our God?" (Psalm 18:31) ". . . [F]or thy name's sake lead me and guide me . . ." (Psalm 31:3).

Words of wisdom

The classic three stages of the spiritual life are: the purgative way (eliminating sins), the illuminative way (replacing sin with virtue), and the unitive way (mystical union with God).

To do

Don't shut out or downplay any of your everyday "God experiences" as you live the adventure of the virtues. The female mystics in particular were very good at following God's lead in their lives. Read *Enduring Grace* (on female mystics) by Carol Flinders.

To journal

What are some experiences you've had with God that you've doubted were real? How did you overcome your doubt?

Prayer

Dear Jesus, help me realize that everyone is called to be a mystic, including me, and it requires loving You with my whole mind, heart, and soul, and loving my neighbor as myself.

July 5

I am the Gardener of your soul. I will make you flower and bear fruit.

God's word

"I am a rose of Sharon, a lily of the valleys" (Song of Songs 2:1). "He who abides in me, and I in him, he it is that bears much fruit . . ." (John 15:5). "And other seeds fell into good soil and brought forth grain . . ." (Mark 4:8).

Words of wisdom

St. Teresa of Avila thought of her soul as a garden. She also described four progressive stages of prayer as different ways in which a garden can be watered: drawing water from a well, using an aqueduct, irrigating from a stream, and rain. Notice how the labor level decreases as we let God get more involved!

To do

Research the traditional "Mary Garden," where various flowers representing various virtues of Jesus and Mary were planted. Which "flower virtues" are your favorites? Start your own Mary Garden!

To journal

How would you describe the garden of your soul? Are you doing some major work tending your garden: pulling out weeds of vices and planting flowers of virtue?

Prayer

Dear Jesus, I am Your garden where You cultivate Your own goodness. May I be good soil.

July 6

When I was born, the Christmas angels sang, "Peace on earth to people of goodwill!"

God's word

"Glory to God in the highest, and on earth peace among men with whom he is pleased!" (Luke 2:14)

Words of Wisdom

Virtue ethics is a branch of moral philosophy based on character rather than on rules or outcomes. This type of ethics was known to the ancient Greeks and medieval philosophers, and was revived in the twentieth century. If you're interested in philosophy, check it out!

To do

Learn more about the Focolare Movement which is Catholic-based, but seeks to unite together all people of goodwill. Pray the "Gloria" from the Mass. Read *The Art of Living* by Epictetus, translated by Sharon Lebell.

To journal

What virtues do you think are needed by those who work for social justice?

Prayer

Dear Jesus, You are so much more than just a great moral teacher—You are God. Yet You said, "He that is not against us is for us" (Mark 9:40). Open my eyes to welcome goodness everywhere in everyone, including Your secular "saints."

July 7

Virtues have no existence apart from those who practice them. My saints are your sure guides!

God's word

"Love the LORD, all you his saints!" (Psalm 31:23) "[G]iving thanks to the Father, who has qualified us to share in the inheritance of the saints in light" (Colossians 1:12). ". . . [T]he smoke of the incense rose with the prayers of the saints . . ." (Revelation 8:4).

Words of wisdom

The saints are our guides through the virtues. As you learn their stories, pay special attention to the obstacles they faced in practicing virtue.

To do

Check out the "Saint a Day" app at www.downloadsforcatholics.com. Get a daily saint book like *Spiritual Advice from the Saints* by Daughters of St. Paul, *Saints of the Roman Calendar* by Enzo Lodi, or the most comprehensive, *Butler's Lives of the Saints* by Alban Butler.

To journal

Saints are not canonized just because of miracles performed through their intercession. Their lives must be examples of heroic virtue. What are the heroic virtues of your favorite saints?

Prayer

Dear Jesus, virtue is attractive even to those who oppose it or persecute it. Herod felt the attraction of Your words. If I have to be a "sign of contradiction" to the world, so be it.

July 8

My Holy Spirit enabled the saints to practice virtue. My Holy Spirit, the saints, and the virtues are inseparable!

God's word

". . . [T]he fruit of the Spirit is love, joy, peace, patience, kindness, goodness, faithfulness, gentleness, self-control . . ." (Galatians 5:22). ". . . [N]o one can say 'Jesus is Lord' except by the Holy Spirit" (1 Corinthians 12:3).

Words of wisdom

The Church has traditionally named twelve fruits of the Spirit (search online for them). Pick a fruit a month to ask the Holy Spirit for.

To do

Watch the movie *Millions* about a little boy who talks to the saints and tries to be good.

To journal

All the saints were able to be what they were and do what they did because they cooperated with grace, with the action of the Holy Spirit in them. What have you been enabled to be and do by cooperating with grace? What would you be patron saint of? (Something you love? Something you excel at? Something you struggle with?)

Prayer

Dear Jesus, virtue is a true escape from the ugliness of sin. Help me be like the saints who, through their virtues, created a little bit of paradise on earth.

July 9

The virtue of prudence is the practical wisdom to know the wisest, most effective thing to do in every circumstance from among a selection of possible good choices.

God's Word

"I, wisdom, live with prudence, and I attain knowledge and discretion" (Proverbs 8:12 NRSV).

Words of Wisdom

"Prudence doesn't mean stifling the Spirit! If the saints had been only naturally prudent, they would never have accomplished great things for God. Look at the crucifix and ask: 'Was this prudent?' Let love decide and direct." (Mother Marie Bernadette Mertens, IHM, www.sistersihmofwichita.org)

To Do

Learn about St. Catherine of Siena, mediator between warring factions, counselor to the pope, good friend, model citizen, Doctor of the Church, and mystic. Learn about St. John Fisher, martyr-bishop of England, who recognized King Henry VIII's intention to destroy marriage and persecute the Catholic Church (while others did not) and resisted.

To Journal

How can you offer good counsel to others? How can you resist dissembling when you are persecuted for your faith?

Prayer

St. Catherine of Siena and St. John Fisher, pray for us!

July 10

The virtue of temperance is balance and moderation in all things, especially regarding your bodily life.

God's word

"Many have died of gluttony, but he who is careful to avoid it prolongs his life" (Sirach 37:31).

Words of Wisdom

It has been said: "No one was ever canonized for being balanced." This may be true, but some *weren't* canonized because they *lacked* the virtue of temperance (e.g., Origen, a Father of the Church).

To do

Learn about Maria Teresa Quevedo from Spain, who enjoyed tennis and entertainment, but also prayer and devotion to God. Learn about Mother Thecla Merlo, an Italian who co-founded the Daughters of St. Paul. She believed in hard work, but also spent time writing to her sisters all over the world and making up jokes and games to enjoy with them.

To journal

How can you balance your lifestyle so that you're not overdoing it in one area? Do you make time for all the important things: prayer, family, friends, leisure, exercise, sleep, learning, work, works of charity, and hobbies? Do you have your priorities straight?

Prayer

Maria Teresa and Mother Thecla, intercede for us!

July 11

The virtue of fortitude is standing firm in the good, especially when you're faced with dire circumstances.

God's Word

"Be strong and of good courage; be not frightened, neither be dismayed; for the LORD your God is with you wherever you go" (Joshua 1:9).

Words of Wisdom

"Our Lord needs courageous young people. It's not always easy to follow God's will in your life, but it's always worth the effort. Since without Christ you can do nothing, the secret lies in clinging to Him with all your might. He will never let you down." (Sr. Cristela MacKinnon, S.de M., www.maryhealth.com)

To Do

Learn about early Christian martyrs Sts. Felicity and Perpetua from North Africa who had every opportunity to deny Christ and live, but didn't. (Felicity was eight months pregnant when first incarcerated.) Learn about British foundress, Mary Ward, who founded a congregation of active religious women when Sisters were only allowed to be cloistered.

To journal

What obstacles in your life cause you to shrink back? What fears do you need to overcome?

Prayer

St. Felicity, St. Perpetua, and Mary Ward, intercede for us!

July 12

The virtue of justice is giving each one his or her due, according to their human dignity and My divine law.

God's word

". . . [L]et justice roll down like waters, and righteousness like an ever-flowing stream" (Amos 5:24).

Words of wisdom

"Justice means to be in right relationship. How does one promote justice? It seems so overwhelming, but, when I look at being in right relationship with myself (purchasing from "just" sources, taking care of my health), with God (spending time in prayer, receiving Holy Communion, reading Scripture) with others (maintaining friendships, having conversations, building intimacy, showing compassion), I discover that I am able to promote God's justice in everyday life." (Sr. Mary Ann Spanjers, OSF, www.fscc-calledtobe.org)

To do

Learn about American Sr. Dorothy Stang, defender of landless people in Brazil, who was murdered in 2005. Learn about Austrian Franz Jagerstatter, husband and father, who resisted conscription into the Nazi army.

To journal

The seven main areas of Catholic social teaching are: human life and dignity, the common good, human rights and responsibilities, the poor, the world of work, peace and justice, and the environment. Which areas do you feel most drawn to? Why?

Prayer

Sr. Dorothy Stang and Bl. Franz Jagerstatter, intercede for us!

July 13

*The virtue of faith is also a gift, a journey, an unshakeable conviction.
It is the first step in our relationship.*

God's word

"He who through faith is righteous shall live" (Romans 1:17).
"And without faith it is impossible to please him . . ." (Hebrews
11:6).

Words of Wisdom

"Faith is trusting God no matter what happens, no matter how
crazy the situation looks, believing that He has a loving plan that can
take anything and make something good come from it!" (Sr. Mary
Michael Huseman, OSF, www.panhandlefranciscans.org)

To do

Learn about the journey of faith of Denmark's Bl. Niels Stensen,
founder of the science of geology. Learn about the acts of faith made
by Japan's St. Paul Miki and companions, Korea's St. Andrew Kim
and companions, China's St. Augustine Zhao Rong and companions,
and Congo's Bl. Isidore Bakanja.

To journal

How do you practice the virtue of faith? How do you *need* to
practice it? Who is your example? How are you an example?

Prayer

Bl. Niels, St. Paul, St. Andrew, St. Augustine, and Bl. Isidore,
pray for us!

July 14

The virtue of hope is trust in My promises.

 "Do not let those who wait for you be put to shame . . ." (Psalm 25:3 NRSV).

 Keep your gaze fixed on Jesus, who is the only true anchor for your soul. Viktor Frankl was a Holocaust survivor, whose book, *Man's Search for Meaning,* has touched and changed countless lives. Find meaning in your suffering and remain steadfast in hope, like he did.

Learn about African-American Sr. Thea Bowman who lived her life overcoming obstacles with zest and song. Learn about Frenchman St. Louis de Montfort, who was teased for his great devotion to Mary, but knew that his books about Mary would do much good after his death.

What gets you discouraged? What makes you doubt God's promises? Get a book of Catholic Bible Promises to write out, memorize, and pray with.

Sr. Thea and St. Louis de Montfort, intercede for us!

July 15

The virtue of love is the meaning and purpose of life. I am meaning and purpose. I am Life. I am Love.

God's Word

". . . I will show you a still more excellent way" (1 Corinthians 12:31). ". . . [T]he greatest of these is love" (1 Corinthians 13:13).

Words of Wisdom

Albanian by birth, Bl. Mother Teresa served the poorest of the poor in India. Often she would refuse money for her work and, instead, invite the would-be giver to serve the poor so that he or she could experience firsthand the joy of loving. Find ways to do hands-on charity to experience this joy!

To Do

Watch *Mother Teresa* starring Olivia Hussey. Although Mother Teresa was admired the world over, she was also criticized for not taking on systemic evil on a large scale. In the film, does it emerge that Mother Teresa actually *has* a philosophy that challenges systemic evil?

To Journal

How do you practice the virtue of love? How do you *need* to practice it? Who is your example? How are you an example?

Prayer

Bl. Mother Teresa, pray for us!

July 16

The virtue of joy is exuberant elation over Me and My works!

God's Word

". . . [T]hat they may have my joy fulfilled in themselves" (John 17:13). ". . . [N]o one will take your joy from you" (John 16:22). "Rejoice in the Lord always; again I will say, Rejoice" (Philippians 4:4). ". . . [T]he stars . . . shone with gladness for him who made them" (Baruch 3:34).

Words of Wisdom

Spain's St. Teresa of Avila loved to dance and rejoice with her sisters before "His Majesty," as she liked to call God. She had a great sense of humor and celebration in life. While enjoying a meal she said, "There's a time for penance and a time for partridge." Once as she enjoyed a piece of fruit she said: "God prepared this piece of fruit from all eternity just for me." Make room for joy in your spirituality.

To Do

A way to joy is contained in this acronym: Jesus Others Yourself.

To journal

How do you practice the virtue of joy? How do you *need* to practice it? Who is your example? How are you an example?

Prayer

St. Teresa of Avila, pray for us!

July 17

The virtue of peace is also My gift. It is personal, and begins in the human heart and spreads out to the world.

God's word

". . . [M]y peace I give to you; not as the world gives do I give to you" (John 14:27).

Words of wisdom

"A simple way to spread peace is through the apostolate of the smile. If you give Jesus and His peace to all you pass by through your smile, you'll be like Our Lady on the way to her cousin Elizabeth. Give a smile and peace enters the human heart." (Sr. Sharon Elizabeth, VHM, www.toledovisitation.org)

To do

Learn about St. Pius X who literally died of a broken heart the day World War I broke out—a tragedy he strove valiantly to avert. Learn about Chicago's Brother Bill Tomes who puts his own body in between the sides in rival gang warfare. Check out: www.catholic-peacefellowship.org.

To journal

How do you practice the virtue of peace? How do you *need* to practice it? Who is your example? How are you an example?

Prayer

St. Pius X, pray for us!

July 18

The virtue of patience is waiting on Me to act when there is nothing more you can do. It is accepting the amount of time it takes to get things done.

God's Word

"By your endurance you will gain your lives" (Luke 21:19). ". . . [C]lothe yourselves with compassion . . . meekness, and patience" (Colossians 3:12 NRSV).

Words of Wisdom

North African St. Monica prayed thirty-two years for her son, Augustine, to be converted. He became one of the greatest writers and Doctors of the Church. Holland's St. Peter Canisius, SJ, dialogued with confused Catholics in Germany during the Reformation. Vietnamese Cardinal Van Thuan was imprisoned by Communists and suffered much for thirteen years. His experience made him more patient than ever. Learn patience from these saints.

To do

Read *St. Monica: The Power of a Mother's Love* by Giovanni Falbo, or *Road of Hope: A Gospel from Prison* by Cardinal Nguyen Van Thuan.

To journal

During the Easter Vigil on Holy Saturday, when the priest prepares the paschal candle and puts the present year on it, he says, "All time belongs to Him." What does that mean to you?

Prayer

St. Monica, St. Peter Canisius, and Cardinal Van Thuan, intercede for us!

July 19

The virtue of kindness is going out of your way to comfort and provide for someone. It is being attentive. It is a way of life that often shows itself in little things.

God's Word

"What do you want me to do for you?" (Mark 10:51) ". . . [T]he mother of Jesus said to him, 'They have no wine'" (John 2:3).

Words of Wisdom

Bl. Margaret of Costello, of Italian nobility, was born blind, deformed, and lame. After confinement and neglect, she was abandoned. She eventually became a Dominican who cared for the poor and prisoners. Bl. Pierre Toussaint, a former Haitian slave, was a hairdresser to the rich and famous of his day in New York City. He refused to carry gossip between clients. Learn kindness from these holy people.

To Do

Practice three little acts of kindness today. It doesn't matter if they go unrecognized—you have blessed the world! Read *Conspiracy of Kindness* by Steve Sjogren.

To Journal

Sometimes those who are treated with cruelty become the kindest people. Do you know someone like this? What's their story?

Prayer

Bl. Margaret and Bl. Pierre, pray for us!

July 20

The virtue of goodness is seeing My love reflected everywhere, even if not apparent, and acting upon it. It is being that reflection of My goodness yourself.

God's word

". . . [O]vercome evil with good" (Romans 12:21).

Words of wisdom

"I used to get angry at those who attacked the Church. But when I realized what these people are doing to their own souls, I began to feel pity, and began to pray for them as well as for those they might lead astray." (Sr. Margaret Mary Mitchel, OSF, www.ssfpa.org)

To do

Learn about eleven-year-old Italian St. Maria Goretti. A martyr of chastity, she resisted an attacker because of concern for his soul. She said, "Stop! It's a sin! You'll go to hell!" It wasn't just this one act that made Maria a saint. She was also known for her kindness and generosity within her family, and great devotion to Jesus in the Eucharist. Watch the film *Fourteen Flowers of Pardon*.

To journal

How do you practice the virtue of goodness? How do you *need* to practice it? Who is your example? How are you an example?

Prayer

St. Maria Goretti, pray for us!

July 21

The virtue of long-suffering is accepting your sufferings—hardships, stress, and problems of all kinds—and offering them up to Me.

God's word

"And let us not grow weary in well-doing . . ." (Galatians 6:9).

Words of wisdom

Suffering well is such an art. A positive attitude helps everyone: ourselves first, and then everyone who has to listen to us!

To do

Learn about Native American St. Kateri Tekakwitha who suffered health problems, the loss of her parents, and persecution for her Catholic faith. Despite her sufferings, Kateri worked hard, prayed much before the Blessed Sacrament, and drew others to Jesus with her gift for story-telling. She loved to pray the Rosary and placed little crosses on the trees in the woods. St. Kateri is the patroness of ecology and the environment (which also experiences long-suffering).

To journal

How do you practice the virtue of long-suffering? How do you *need* to practice it? Who is your example? How are you an example?

Prayer

St. Kateri Tekakwitha, pray for us!

July 22

The virtue of gentleness is tenderness toward all of My creation, even toward those who are not gentle.

God's Word

"But we were gentle among you, like a nurse taking care of her children" (1 Thessalonians 2:7).

Words of Wisdom

St. Francis of Assisi (Italy) was so gentle that he would move earthworms to the side of the road so they wouldn't get trampled! He showed great care for lepers and the poor. But St. Francis hadn't always put gentleness into action. He was a wealthy young partygoer who decided to take seriously Jesus's life and teachings, and thus became one of the most Christ-like figures in history. Consider what needs conversion in your life.

To do

Watch *Francis of Assisi* starring Bradford Dillman as Francis and Dolores Hart as Clare. Watch *Little Flowers of St. Francis* directed by Roberto Rossellini, starring real Italian Franciscans!

To journal

Why do so many Christians reject gentleness? How do they justify their lack of gentleness? How do you live gentleness?

Prayer

"Make me a channel of your peace. Where there is hatred, let me sow love. Where there is injury, pardon." (Prayer of St. Francis)

July 23

The virtue of faithfulness (fidelity) is constant devotion to Me, others to whom you are committed, and your duties in life.

God's word

"Be faithful unto death, and I will give you the crown of life" (Revelation 2:10).

Words of wisdom

"Fidelity is tough. To persevere in seeking and doing the will of God, daily and for life, takes uncommon determination, not to mention grace. In the end, fidelity glorifies God by the person it shapes: someone resembling Him, whose presence brings His presence, and who loves with His love." (Sr. Bernarda Seferovich, O.Cist., www.nunocist.org)

To do

Learn about St. Joan of Arc. She was faithful to her mission till the end. In the midst of armed conflict and underhanded politics she became a prisoner and bargaining chip of the powerful. Although hardly any loyalty was shown to her, she remained faithful to everyone and everything that was her responsibility. She was burned at the stake at only nineteen years of age.

To journal

Who has claims on your faithfulness? What promises have you made and to whom? What are your duties and responsibilities? What helps you to be faithful?

Prayer

St. Joan of Arc, pray for us!

July 24

The virtue of modesty is chastity (purity) in action. Chastity is an interior and exterior virtue, whereas modesty is more concerned with the exterior.

God's word

". . . [T]hose parts of the body which we think less honourable we invest with the greater honor, and our unpresentable parts are treated with greater modesty . . ." (1 Corinthians 12:23).

Words of wisdom

Modesty differs by culture. Because we live in a fallen world, we must conduct ourselves in a modest manner. It is because our bodies are good that we cover them, not because they're bad!

To do

There's no need to wear long sleeves and long dresses in order to be modest. If you're truly practicing chastity, you'll know how to dress. Dressing a particular way doesn't make you modest, and doesn't necessarily help someone else to be chaste (because chastity starts as an inside job)!

To journal

Do I love my body? Am I comfortable with it? Do I see God's glory in my body?

Prayer

Dear Jesus, help me be comfortable in my own skin. Never let me separate my person from my body so that I will always have respect for my whole self.

July 25

The virtue of self-control is always choosing what is good for body and soul together.

God's Word

"For everything there is a season, and a time for every matter under heaven" (Ecclesiastes 3:1).

Words of wisdom

"The practice of self-control should be considered an expression of love, whereby we freely conform our will to the will of God. Self-control is a joyful transformation pleasing to an intimate and personal God." (Mother Susan Rueve, OSF, www.divineteacher.org)

To do

Learn about St. Margaret of Cortona (Italy). Beautiful, affectionate, and passionate, Margaret followed her heart, which eventually led her to the heart of God. Although others looked down on her, she trusted that God would help her order her desires. Watch *Babette's Feast*.

To journal

"Know thyself." Self-control doesn't always mean sacrificing something. It simply means knowing one's own nature, and having the mind, will, heart, and body in integrated harmony—not having one or the other dominate in excessive or sinful ways. What parts of yourself do you feel you need to know better? How will you go about knowing yourself better?

Prayer

St. Margaret of Cortona, pray for us!

July 26

The virtue of chastity (purity) is seeing My glory in the human body.

God's Word

". . . [A] body you have prepared for me" (Hebrews 10:5 NRSV).

Words of Wisdom

Don't confuse chastity with celibacy. Celibacy is abstaining from sexual activity. Everyone who is not married is called to celibacy, but everyone, including the married, is called to chastity. Chastity is the integration of soul and body in holiness.

To Do

Learn about the married couple, Luigi and Maria Quatrocchi, Blesseds in the Church. Luigi was attorney general of Italy, and Maria was an educator, writer, and activist. They had four children and were married fifty years. Learn about St. Theodora, Empress of the Byzantine Empire, who venerated holy icons in secret (her husband, the Emperor, was an iconoclast). She was instrumental in convening the Second Council of Nicaea, which taught that God *can* be represented in art because in the Incarnation the Word became flesh, a body that can be represented.

To Journal

How do you practice the virtue of chastity? How do you *need* to practice it? Who is your example? How are you an example?

Prayer

Bl. Luigi, Bl. Maria, and St. Theodora, pray for us!

July 27

The virtue of poverty is simplicity of spirit that is content with having basic needs met. It is also using this world's goods to produce, provide, preserve, and conserve for others. It is trusting in My Divine Providence.

God's Word

"Blessed are the poor in spirit . . ." (Matthew 5:3).

Words of Wisdom

St. Katherine Drexel, born in 1858 into an extremely wealthy family of Philadelphia, saw the needs of blacks and Native Americans, and began donating money to help them. She realized that a religious congregation was needed to serve these peoples. She told the pope about it, and he told her *she* should start one—not what she wanted to hear! But she did: The Sisters of the Blessed Sacrament. She donated her entire inheritance of twenty million dollars to further the works of her sisters. Remember that we often need to put our money where our mouth is, or our mouth where our money is!

To do

Learn about Simone Weil, a philosopher by profession, who chose to share the hard life of the French workers in World War II France.

To journal

What would you do with twenty million dollars?

Prayer

St. Katherine Drexel and Simone Weil, intercede for us!

July 28

The virtue of obedience is first of all listening, then embracing My ways.

God's word

". . . [T]o obey is better than sacrifice . . ." (1 Samuel 15:22).

Words of Wisdom

Henri de Lubac (France) developed a deepening of the Catholic faith leading up to Vatican II. The Council was not only about renewing for the future *(aggiornamento),* but also reviving ancient Christian practices *(ressourcement).* His work was not accepted and he was ordered by the Church not to publish anything on certain controversial subjects. He humbly obeyed. After Vatican II—which came to the same conclusions he had—he was made a cardinal by Pope John Paul II.

To do

St. Faustina and St. Padre Pio were both religious and, despite the extraordinary gifts God had given them (both were visionaries), saw obedience as their way of holiness. Reflect on how you put obedience into practice in your life.

To journal

Speaking to religious, John Paul II said, "Obedience is the sharpest of the three gold nails that nail religious to the cross with Christ." Why do you think he said that? Would that be true for you?

Prayer

St. Faustina, St. Padre Pio, and Cardinal Henri de Lubac, intercede for us!

July 29

The virtue of generosity is availability and bigness of heart in giving of oneself.

God's word

". . . [T]he righteous gives and does not hold back" (Proverbs 21:26). "[G]ive and it will be given to you; good measure, pressed down, shaken together, running over . . ." (Luke 6:38).

Words of wisdom

"St. Martha exemplifies generosity in action. However, our Lord admonished her perhaps because she was acting for the wrong reason. Let us be Marthas ready to jump in and serve our Lord, but with generous and loving hearts." (Sr. Maria Gemma Martek, OP, www.sistersofmary.org)

To do

Learn about St. Paul. He was specially called to bring Jesus's name to "kings and nations," but he could have responded any way he wanted: by doing a little bit of good, a moderate amount of good, or by reaching a large portion of the world with the Gospel.

To journal

How do you practice the virtue of generosity? How do you *need* to practice it? Who is your example? How are you an example?

Prayer

St. Martha and St. Paul the Apostle, pray for us!

July 30

Humility is truth. I have given you gifts and talents. You also have negative qualities. Humility is acknowledging the truth of both these realities.

God's Word

"... [G]lorify yourself with humility, and ascribe to yourself honour according to your worth" (Sirach 10:28).

Words of Wisdom

False humility is denying that we've been given talents and gifts. Pride is acting as though our talents and gifts are from ourselves. If we are prone to false humility, we need to rally our courage to use our God-given gifts. If we are prone to pride, we need to be truly humble.

To do

St. Juan Diego, although chosen to see and speak with Our Lady, didn't think he was important and was more interested in helping his dying uncle than having visions! St. Peter the Apostle recognized his sinfulness in the presence of Jesus: "Depart from me, for I am a sinful man, O Lord" (Luke 5:8). Today, name the good and the bad that is in you.

To journal

Which do you need to work on more: overcoming false humility or overcoming pride? Why? How will you go about it?

Prayer

St. Juan Diego and St. Peter the Apostle, pray for us!

July 31

The virtue of forgiveness is really more than a virtue. It is an essential way of life and the reason why I came to earth.

God's Word

"Forgive your brother from your heart" (Matthew 18:35).

Words of Wisdom

"True forgiveness is possible only with the Lord's grace. It may often seem beyond our capability, but ask the Lord for the gift of a forgiving heart. Meditate on Jesus's mercy and forgiveness, especially as you look on the crucifix. Try then to forgive your brother or sister in the same way." (Sr. M. Beata, FSGM, www.altonfranciscans. org)

To do

Learn about the 2006 shooting of Amish school girls in Pennsylvania, and how the Amish families immediately forgave the perpetrator (who killed himself), and reached out to his widow and family. Learn about Corrie ten Boom (active in the Dutch resistance during WWII) and her forgiveness of the Nazi who killed her sister. Learn about Pope John Paul II's meeting with and forgiveness of the man who shot him.

To journal

How can forgiveness become a way of life for you?

Prayer

"Forgive us our trespasses, as we forgive those who trespass against us."

August 1

I made you as a unity of body and soul, a spiritualized body and an embodied spirit. You do not have a body and soul, you are a body and soul!

God's word

". . . [T]he LORD God formed man of dust . . . and breathed into his nostrils the breath of life . . ." (Genesis 2:7).

Words of wisdom

The secular and religious worlds both struggle with the body. The body is often seen as less important than the soul, or bad because it is material. But the material world is good. God created it. Because the body is spiritualized, one with our soul, John Paul II said, "The body can never be reduced to mere matter."

To do

The body expresses the soul. Reflect on your "bodyliness." We're always expressing our soul through our body. What's your favorite way? Dance? Sports? Arts? Cooking? Helping? Memorize this definition: A human person is a body and soul, together forever.

To journal

Write a short history of your attitude toward your body: growth, agility, sleep, food, sexuality, body-image, sickness, disability, etc.

Prayer

Dear Jesus, help me live and love my "bodyliness." Give me a new understanding and appreciation of who I am as body and soul.

August 2

There are two different ways to be a body, to be a person: male and female. Together you are the human race, made to complete and complement each other.

"Male and female he created them, and he blessed them . . ." (Genesis 5:2).

What is John Paul II's ground-breaking theology of the body? It is a whole new starting point for human beings to understand the meaning of life through God's plan for the human person—body and soul—revealed through the body.

Familiarize yourself with *Man and Woman He Created Them: A Theology of the Body*, and *Theology of the Body Explained* by Christopher West.

Theology of the body is also a Bible study, taking us from Genesis to Revelation. It begins with the earthly marriage of Adam and Eve, and ends with the heavenly marriage of the Lamb (Jesus the Bridegroom and his bride, the Church). What is God telling us?

Dear Jesus, thank you for inspiring John Paul the Great to teach this incredible synthesis of the wisdom of creation, Scripture, and Church teaching to heal our world!

August 3

It is a life-long journey to understand what is real. It is a life-changing journey to live in accord with reality.

God's word

"And they shall all be taught by God" (John 6:45).

Words of Wisdom

Theology of the body is the long-awaited reply to the mind/body split that has been ravaging our culture for the past five hundred years. Influential French philosopher René Descartes went so far as to say that the only thing he could be sure existed was his mind, thus denigrating the entire material world.

To do

Can you think of ways the mind/body split has affected history, religion, science, and you?

To journal

What would the world be like if people really believed that bodies are as important as souls? That the body is sacred?

Prayer

Dear Jesus, even people who seem to value the body may only value it for one aspect: pleasure, beauty, "spare parts," or treat it like a machine, a possession. Help us regain an understanding of the whole rich truth about the body.

August 4

You are a mystery—like Me! But I have revealed our mystery insofar as you are able to comprehend it.

God's word

". . . [T]hat through the church the manifold wisdom of God might now be made known . . ." (Ephesians 3:10).

Words of wisdom

Many theologies and philosophies of the body are circulating around. Since we are all affected by these viewpoints, we need to be deeply rooted in what God has revealed to us.

To do

Find out about the following beliefs on the body: Puritanism, hedonism, Manichaeism, Gnosticism, scientism, Hinduism, Buddhism, and the Greek philosophies.

To journal

Reflect on what you have read so far about theology of the body. What are your main questions? How do you think it might help you?

Prayer

Dear Jesus, we are just beginning to unpack this wonderful new gift of theology of the body. Many of our ancestors lived it without having the words to explain it. Today we are in such need of this understanding because of the sexual revolution, media, technology, and science. Please enlighten our world.

August 5

How did the human race come to be? One day you will know!

God's word

"My frame was not hidden from you, when I was being made in secret, intricately woven in the depths of the earth" (Psalm 139:15 NRSV).

Words of Wisdom

Can Catholics believe in evolution? Evolution is a natural process by which things change. Did our bodies evolve from a different species? Perhaps. If so, at one point in time, God directly infused the now-human body with an immortal soul, and directly infuses all subsequent human bodies with souls.

To do

Do you have a sufficient understanding of the basic science and theology surrounding the origins of human life? Do you know how our Catholic understanding differs from that of fundamentalist Christians who take the Bible literally? From those who believe in a Godless evolution?

To journal

God could have made human life unfold in many ways. What are some amazing things about the human body that you find fascinating?

Prayer

Dear Jesus, science is the study of "who, what, when, where, and how," and theology is the study of "why." Help both fields realize they're not opposed, because they both seek truth.

August 6

I have given human beings intelligence and freedom. Will you follow My plan? Will you uphold human dignity and the dignity of all creation?

God's Word

"The LORD God took the man and put him in the garden of Eden to till it and keep it" (Genesis 2:15).

Words of Wisdom

Oftentimes, people think because they *can* do something, they should. But human actions have to be guided by natural law, human law, and divine law, which uphold the integrity of each thing as it is in itself.

To do

Read *Abolition of Man* by C. S. Lewis. What does the title mean? Watch the original *Jurassic Park*. What lessons can be learned from it for the future?

To journal

What do you think about "participatory evolution"—that is, humans participating in their own evolution through processes like genetic engineering? This is not just about genetically curing diseases, but enhancing, for example, human intelligence. (Remember, this manipulation is often done on people at the earliest stages of life who have no choice about it.)

Prayer

Dear Jesus, help us, the human family, be in right relationship to ourselves, and act responsibly toward future generations.

August 7

Each human being is a profound mystery of infinite worth.

God's word

"For the Spirit searches everything, even the depths of God. For what person knows a man's thoughts except the spirit of the man which is in him? So also no one comprehends the thoughts of God except the Spirit of God" (1 Corinthians 2:10–11).

Words of wisdom

We live at three different levels simultaneously: the natural, the human, and the supernatural. We are not just biological animals, we are not just unique human animals; we are called to divinization in Jesus Christ! And our bodies, which are matter, share in all three levels! St. Basil once said, "Man is an animal who has received the vocation to become God."

To do

How does God use matter to come to us and transform us? Pray for the grace to experience God more in material things. Read *Why Matter Matters* by David Lang.

To journal

How does God bless you through creation? What is your experience of the physicality of the sacraments?

Prayer

Dear Jesus, through the sacraments You unite matter, word, and spirit. Help me not see them as only spiritual, but help me rejoice in their "earthiness"!

August 8

I created humans to unite the material and spiritual worlds. You are a cosmic marvel! Can you tell that I love matter? I made lots of it.

God's Word

"[W]hat are human beings that you are mindful of them . . . ? Yet you have made them a little lower than God" (Psalm 8:4–5 NRSV).

Words of Wisdom

One of the most important words we can define is "person." Angels and humans are persons because God—who made them like Himself—is a Person, or rather a Trinity of Persons. Persons are able to think, will, and love. "Person" is hard to define because of the mystery inherent in persons.

To do

Without God, persons will eventually turn on themselves. Read *The Drama of Atheist Humanism* by Henri de Lubac or *Architects of the Culture of Death* by Donald DeMarco.

To journal

Who in your life has been an example of how to treat persons? Who makes you feel cherished? People don't remember what you said or how you said it—only how you make them feel.

Prayer

Dear Jesus, I want to approach every person with respect and awe at all times because of who they are in You and their infinite value!

August 9

Your human body has a history: from its humble beginnings as dust, to My Incarnation, to My Ascension, to your future glorification with Me!

God's Word

"When shall I come and behold the face of God?" (Psalm 42:2)

Words of Wisdom

From Pope John Paul II we learn that only Jesus Christ reveals the whole truth about man, and that Jesus is the human face of God and the divine face of man. The Bible tells us we are made from dust and science tells us we, along with the whole universe, are made from stardust (hydrogen)!

To do

God now has a human face. What is your favorite depiction of the face of Jesus? Learn about the recently recovered Veil of Manoppello that seems to match the Shroud of Turin. Could this be the face of Jesus on Easter morning? Put a picture of the face of Jesus on your computer or cell phone's wallpaper.

To journal

How have you found your true self—body and soul—in Jesus?

Prayer

Dear Jesus, glory to You for the indescribable gift of Yourself, true God and true man.

August 10

I have revealed to you My innermost nature and secret: I am continuously making a gift of Myself in an eternal exchange of love.

God's Word

". . . I lay down my life, that I may take it again. No one takes it from me, but I lay it down of my own accord" (John 10:17–18).

Words of Wisdom

How are humans fulfilled? It's very simple. Humans are only fulfilled when they make a gift of themselves. This gift is made through the body.

To Do

Read Pope Benedict's encyclical *God Is Love*. Note how it builds on theology of the body. Write out number 221 of the *Catechism of the Catholic Church*.

To Journal

We are called to love as God loves, but before Jesus, we didn't fully understand how God loves. How do you love as God loves?

Prayer

Dear Jesus, thank You for choosing to expand Your inner life of love to include us, to include me, by Your total gift, laying down Your life on the altar of the cross.

August 11

Do you know that your body has a spousal meaning? Your body reveals that I made you for union!

God's word

"'. . . [T]he two shall become one flesh.' This mystery is a profound one, and I am saying that it refers to Christ and the church" (Ephesians 5:31–32).

Words of wisdom

Not everyone will express the spousal meaning of their bodies by getting married, but everyone is called to union with God and others. How are you making (and planning to make) a total gift of self? This is largely done through one's state in life. In what smaller, everyday ways do you make a gift of self?

To do

How do you live the "complementarity of the sexes" in your encounters and friendships with members of the opposite sex? Are you trying to understand and appreciate their differences as "the other"?

To journal

What do you like most about men? What do you find most puzzling? What do you like least?

Prayer

Dear Jesus, humans are not just male and female on the biological level: we complement each other spiritually, emotionally, psychologically, and socially. Thank You for making us in Your image with a forever future!

August 12

I created men and women different but equal, similar but not identical.
You can get insight into the purpose of something by its design.

God's Word

"Therefore a man leaves his father and his mother and cleaves to his wife, and they become one flesh" (Genesis 2:24).

Words of Wisdom

A symphony is beautiful because all the instruments are different and yet they harmonize. Creation is an amazing symphony. Men and women are called to make beautiful music together. *Vive la différence!* John Paul II says that not enough is made of the ordinary love between a married man and woman.

To do

In the Middle Ages, the philosophers admired God's "plentitudinous universe"—full of all different kinds of beings, and saw it as a sign of God's greatness and majesty. What do you love best in God's panoply? Do you need to embrace more of God's diversity?

To journal

Feminists in the 1970s used to decry the statement: "Biology is destiny." What is meant by that statement? How does it make you feel?

Prayer

Dear Jesus, each individual is called to make a gift of self. Thank You that the Trinity is the model of perfect gift for married and single people alike.

August 13

There are those who affirm the body and deny Me. There are those who affirm Me and deny the body. Affirm both.

God's Word

"Take delight in the LORD, and he will give you the desires of your heart" (Psalm 37:4).

Words of wisdom

We do not treat our bodies as hedonists do, but neither do we treat them as stoics do. We are body and soul, a duality in unity, and both are very good. We go to God *through* the desires of soul and body. God gave us these desires because He is going to fulfill them in eternity.

To do

On earth, our desires can be fulfilled according to the virtues, especially the cardinal virtues of prudence, temperance, fortitude, and justice. What desires of mine do I need to engage with these virtues?

To journal

We also deny ourselves when it's for the good of both body and soul. Sometimes we discipline certain desires for a period of time. What desires might I need to deny (partially, temporarily, permanently)? What desires should I *stop* denying (partially, temporarily, permanently)?

Prayer

Dear Jesus, teach me to love both body and soul properly through virtue and prayer.

August 14

I love you so much I want to marry you. Marriage is union. Our union will be perfect, and we will be united in a way you can't even imagine now.

God's word

". . . [T]he marriage of the Lamb has come, and his Bride has made herself ready . . ." (Revelation 19:7).

Words of wisdom

The closest form of love we know is the love of husband and wife. Marriage is also the best way we have to understand how God loves us, because God Himself chose this as the dominant image of His love in the Bible.

To do

In heaven, we will be completely fulfilled in our masculinity and femininity. Read *Crossing the Threshold of Love* by Mary Shivanandan to see how, through marriage, we can be partially fulfilled in this life.

To journal

What are some of your deepest longings you want fulfilled in heaven?

Prayer

Dear Jesus, many of us are uncomfortable with the metaphor of marriage and sexuality as the way you love us, because in a fallen world we often experience them as twisted and broken. But the reason we recognize them as broken is because we have some idea of how it should be. That ideal *can be* on earth and *will be* in heaven, thanks to You.

August 15

In Me, you can be victorious over anything, and not just in a negative way through avoidance.

God's Word

"Sin is crouching at the door; its desire is for you, but you must master it" (Genesis 4:7).

Words of Wisdom

Saints are sinners who never gave up. We can overcome even sexual sin such as masturbation, fornication, adultery, and pornography, in spite of its addictive nature. God is greater than our addictions.

To do

Do you struggle with sexual sin? All sin starts with a good desire that gets twisted. Purity is being able to see the glory of God in the human body, and act accordingly. Get help from a spiritual director or confessor or enroll in a sexual addiction recovery program.

To journal

Sexual sin is not necessarily the worst sin (lack of charity is), but it feels the most shameful because in sexual sin we sin against our own bodies. Even though sexual sin is difficult to overcome, it is possible because Jesus came to redeem us, body and soul. If we deny this, we empty the cross of its meaning and power.

Prayer

Dear Jesus, Your grace is sufficient for me.

August 16

True love always does what's good for the other—even if the other person doesn't always understand what's best.

God's Word

"Let your light so shine before men, that they may see your good works and give glory to your Father who is in heaven" (Matthew 5:16).

Words of Wisdom

Lust is using someone for one's own self-gratification, instead of relating to him or her as a person. Lust can never be "doing what's good for oneself," because lust goes against the dignity of both the user and the used.

To do

Watch *Life Is Beautiful*. What does Guido call Dora throughout the movie? Does he love her or lust after her? How do you know which it is?

To journal

In *Love and Responsibility*, John Paul II says, "Love . . . means just that: to limit one's freedom on behalf of another. Limitation of one's freedom might seem to be something negative and unpleasant, but love makes it a positive, joyful, and creative thing." Comment on this.

Prayer

Dear Jesus, I thank You that every man is a prince and every woman is a princess because we're children of the King!

August 17

When things go to extremes in whatever direction, human beings rebel and so they should.

God's Word

"The body is not meant for immorality, but for the Lord, and the Lord for the body" (1 Corinthians 6:13).

Words of Wisdom

The sexual revolution that began in the 1960s was, in some respects, a rebellion against sexual repression and hypocrisy. But neither repression nor indulgence is good. God's plan is for the *redemption* of the body.

To Do

Research the cause and consequences of the sexual revolution which is still with us today. Read *Margaret Sanger: Father of Modern Society* by Elasah Drogin. Did the sexual revolution deliver on its promises of fulfillment, happiness, authentic relationships, sexual health, fewer unplanned pregnancies, fewer unwanted children, and more respect for women?

To Journal

Can something else fulfill the promises of the sexual revolution? What?

Prayer

Dear Jesus, You want the best for us more than we do. Theology of the body is the new sexual revolution. Help us follow Your plans for true fulfillment.

August 18

I speak to you in words of love and in ways that you'll understand. Listen carefully.

God's Word

"I will open my mouth in a parable . . ." (Psalm 78:2). "Why do you speak to them in parables?" (Matthew 13:10)

Words of Wisdom

There are no wasted words or images in the Bible. Every one is precious and true. However, in our overly-pragmatic, positivistic, "do-it-yourself," "make-it-up-as-you-go-along" culture, people tend to believe that a symbol is just a symbol. But when it comes to biblical symbols, they are the only way to a profound reality and must be taken very seriously!

To do

In *Man and Woman He Created Them,* John Paul II suggests that westerners struggle with theology because our theology uses the language of philosophy. Westerners also struggle with symbols and images in theology. Why do you think that is? Read the prophets Jeremiah and Hosea. Why are these prophets like performance artists?

To journal

What biblical symbols or images really speak to you?

Prayer

Dear Jesus, You have given us Your best in Your word. Help me grasp the meaning of Your images, symbols, and parables.

August 19

Everything has its own language. Love/body/sex has a language all its own. Do you know that language?

God's word

"I adjure you, O daughters of Jerusalem, do not stir up or awaken love until it is ready!" (Song of Songs 8:4 NRSV) "Arise, my love, my fair one, and come away" (Song of Songs 2:10).

Words of wisdom

Love/body/sex language says: *fundamental*—between a man and a woman who relate as persons not things, in love, not lust; *free*—not coerced; *full*—exclusive relationship, total gift, mutual exchange (marriage); *faithful*—permanent commitment; *fruitful*—open to new life (children).

To do

Run pop culture examples or movies about "true love" through "God's Five F's of True Love" listed above. Which ones came out as true love? Which ones didn't?

To journal

If one of the above elements of true love is not present, the language of love/body/sex can be spoken as a lie. But lies can be turned around once the truth is spoken. What are some ways love/body/sex lies can be turned into true love?

Prayer

Dear Jesus, theology of the body can "happen" when entered into as a couple. May all couples find true love.

August 20

Let nature speak to you of its design and essence. Let your body and being speak to you of its design and essence.

God's Word

"I am my beloved's and my beloved is mine" (Song of Songs 6:3).

Words of Wisdom

How can the body, which is corporal, be a theology, which is the study of God, who is spirit? Because the Father created and reveals Himself through our bodies, because Jesus is the Word made flesh, and because we are temples of the Holy Spirit. "Through . . . 'visible' masculinity and femininity . . . the body is capable of making visible what is invisible: the spiritual and divine. It has been created to transfer into the visible reality of the world the mystery hidden from eternity in God, and thus to be a sign of it" (*Man and Woman He Created Them*, 19:4).

To Do

Meditate on the above words, which are the heart of theology of the body.

To Journal

How have those words quoted from *Man and Woman He Created Them* affected you?

Prayer

Dear Jesus, we participate so organically in Your creation. My body is what it is and something greater at the same time. Help me stay in touch with my body and all that it is and means!

August 21

Women have suffered in a particular way since the fall of our first parents.

God's Word

". . . [I]n pain you shall bring forth children, yet your desire shall be for your husband, and he shall rule over you" (Genesis 3:16).

Words of Wisdom

God did not *command* men to dominate women. He predicted it as the sad consequence of original sin. Meditate on Gustave Doré's beautiful illustration *Jesus and the Woman Taken in Adultery*. Jesus is the defender and friend of women.

To Do

Women all over the world are mistreated with indignity and injustice. Customs such as bride burning, female genital mutilation, and honor killings abound. What can you do to help?

To Journal

What is the difference between feminism, radical feminism, and Christian feminism? What constructive contributions has feminism made to women and families? What destructive contributions?

Prayer

Dear Jesus, sadly, women are even oppressed in the name of religion. But in Christianity, men are called to love women "as they love their own bodies" and "as Christ loved the Church" (cf. Ephesians 5:28–29). And You loved the Church by serving her and laying down Your life for her.

August 22

My Gospel is Good News for everyone, especially the poor.

God's Word

". . . [H]e has anointed me to preach good news to the poor. He has sent me to proclaim release to the captives . . . to set at liberty those who are oppressed . . ." (Luke 4:18).

Words of Wisdom

The above Scripture speaks of signs that the Messiah has come. The reference to the poor, captive, and oppressed means physically as well as spiritually. Women could be considered among the poor and captive at the time of Jesus and even now.

To do

Theology of the body is good news for women because when sex is abused, women are the first victims; women and men are equal; all humanity is feminine before God because we're all in the position of receiving from God; and natural family planning (NFP) is completely healthy for women and makes both husband and wife attentive to the woman's cycle. Learn more about NFP.

To journal

Write out the above reasons that theology of the body is good news for women and memorize them!

Prayer

Dear Jesus, thank You for loving us women in a special way.

August 23

I am the one High Priest of the New Covenant. There is only one high priest on whom all priesthood is modeled.

God's Word

". . . [Y]ou are . . . a royal priesthood, a holy nation, God's own people . . ." (1 Peter 2:9).

Words of Wisdom

There are two kinds of priesthood: ministerial (ordained) priesthood and the priesthood of the faithful. So, women *are* priests!

To do

Read the Church documents by John Paul II *On the Dignity and Vocation of Women* and *Ordinatio Sacerdotalis* on the non-ordination of women, and the book, *The Catholic Priesthood and Women* by Sr. Sara Butler. Sr. Sara, an astute theologian, used to be a proponent for women's ordination until John Paul II's writings helped clarify the issue for her.

To journal

What is your vocation and identity as a woman in the Church? How are you exercising your priesthood of the faithful, that is, how are you living your Baptism? How are you imitating Mary?

Prayer

Dear Jesus, we women can and do represent You, just not as *ordained* priests. Thank You, beloved Bridegroom, for making me "another Mary."

August 24

I speak through My Church in every age. Listen to her.

"Behold, I stand at the door and knock; if any one hears my voice and opens the door, I will come in to him and eat with him, and he with me" (Revelation 3:20).

Words of wisdom

The beautiful purpose of sex is inseparably twofold: procreation and the mutual love of the spouses. Every act of marital love (sexual intercourse) must be open to new life. Catholics do things naturally, because God reveals Himself through nature. Scripture and the Church help *interpret* nature for us.

To do

Read *Humanae Vitae*. This tiny Church document continues to cause a huge fuss because it says "no" to artificial contraception. Artificial contraception separates love, body, sex, and fruitfulness (see August 19). Artificial contraception isn't wrong simply because it's artificial (human ingenuity uses lots of artificial things), but because the dignity of marital love and openness to new life must *always* be respected, not just sometimes.

To journal

Note any struggles or questions you have about *Humanae Vitae*. Read *Women, Sex and the Church* by Erika Bachiochi to get answers.

Prayer

Dear Jesus, help us trust You who are Love and Life, not false solutions that leave us empty.

August 25

I have called some to celibacy for the kingdom, for the marriage of the Lamb, the heavenly marriage now. Marriage is a sacrament or sign of the heavenly marriage, whereas celibacy for the kingdom is not a sacrament because it is not a sign, but the real heavenly marriage.

God's word

". . . [T]here are eunuchs who have made themselves eunuchs for the sake of the kingdom of heaven. He who is able to receive this, let him receive it" (Matthew 19:12).

Words of wisdom

Does theology of the body apply to the unmarried? Yes! If you are a body, theology of the body applies to you!

To do

Our world is obsessed with sex, and yet doesn't value sex enough! Our bodies and souls are not made for casual sex. Science proves this. Always question aloud media that show unmarried couples having sex.

To journal

What are some reasons married couples are celibate at times? Some categories of celibate people are the sick, children, elderly, etc. Can they live fulfilled lives? How?

Prayer

Dear Jesus, it's simple, thanks to You. If we're single, we're called to celibacy. Sex is only for the married.

August 26

Answering the call to a life of celibacy may come early in life or later, even after sexual experiences.

God's Word

"For blessed is the barren woman . . . she will have fruit when God examines souls" (Wisdom 3:13). "The fruit of noble struggles is a glorious one . . ." (Wisdom 3:15 NAB).

Words of Wisdom

We are sexual beings, even as celibates! Celibacy is not repression. We live out our sexuality *as* celibates. Sexual energy is channeled into loving and serving in other ways. All men are called to be spiritual fathers, and some are also called to be physical fathers. All women are called to be spiritual mothers, and some are also called to be physical mothers.

To Do

Perform some of the spiritual works of mercy.

To Journal

How can you be more of a spiritual mother? Who can you help spiritually? Who do you know who exemplifies a spiritual mother? Who are your spiritual children? Any one we even simply pray for could be considered a spiritual child.

Prayer

Dear Jesus, You are all about life: the transmission of new life, sustaining life, abundant life, and sharing Your divine life with us for all eternity. Make me all about life, too.

August 27

Sexual identity is very important. Whatever is in need of clarity on earth will be made whole in heaven.

God's word

"Woe to him who strives with his Maker . . . ! Does the clay say to him who fashions it, 'What are you making?'" (Isaiah 45:9)?

Words of wisdom

Theology of the body is good news for every *body,* including hermaphrodites or intersex people. But these bodies, too, are good because everything God makes is good.

To do

God created a good world, not necessarily a perfect world in the limited human understanding of perfect. Watch *March of the Penguins.* Does the design of these penguins seem perfect? What else might God have going on here?

To journal

God loves variety, but humans generally don't, so we often fail to accept and love human beings who are different. Are there different human beings you find harder to love? How can you learn to love them?

Prayer

Dear Jesus, You said, "Be perfect, as your heavenly Father is perfect" (Matthew 5:48). You meant to be perfect in love, especially for those who are different, who are often the "least of these."

August 28

As you let My creation speak to you, remember that this is a fallen world, and that your human nature is fallen. As you listen to nature, you must also listen to Me, and let Me redeem you!

God's Word

"For God sent the Son into the world, not to condemn the world, but that the world might be saved through him" (John 3:17).

Words of wisdom

We don't blindly follow nature, we follow the Creator! We don't blindly follow fallen human nature, we follow the Redeemer! Same-sex attraction is a disorder of our fallen human nature/nurture. It is not sinful in itself, it is only a tendency. Acting out is where sinfulness comes in.

To do

Do you know someone struggling with same-sex attraction? Recommend the Catholic organization Courage (www.couragerc. net). Educate yourself about homosexuality by reading books by Fr. John Harvey, Leanne Payne, Joseph Nicolosi, and Janelle Hallman.

To journal

The French philosopher, Albert Camus, said, "Before you meet a morality, you have to meet a love." What did he mean?

Prayer

Dear Jesus, we may or may not be fully healed of our many disorders in this life, but we can always lead a holy life by Your grace.

August 29

If you love people—which does not mean approving of their actions—you can be a source of strength for them to carry their crosses in life and change for the better. Rejection doesn't help anyone.

God's Word

"Those who are well have no need of a physician, but those who are sick; I came not to call the righteous, but sinners" (Mark 2:17).

Words of Wisdom

Generally, people with same-sex attraction, or who are transgender have fully male or fully female bodies (unlike hermaphrodites/intersex people), but psychologically are attracted to or identify with the opposite sex for many different reasons, known and unknown. We are dealing with the deep mystery of the human person and must tread carefully!

To Do

We can reject people in subtle ways: a scornful look, a negative comment, ridicule, or neglect. Who do you need to accept and reach out to in love?

To Journal

Describe how you can love someone without approving (or even understanding) their actions.

Prayer

Dear Jesus, human laws must uphold natural law and divine law, because that is truly good for us, but the highest law is Your law of love which we are always free to put into practice!

August 30

The sickness, pain, suffering, and death you now experience were not a part of My original plan—they are the result of original sin. But I have transformed them!

God's Word

"Jesus . . . healed them all . . ." (Matthew 12:15). ". . . [N]either shall there be mourning nor crying nor pain any more, for the former things have passed away" (Revelation 21:4).

Words of Wisdom

John Paul II said that the healthy are the more or less healthy, and the sick are the more or less sick, because it can change at any moment, and roles can be reversed! There's nothing like pain to make us know we don't *have* a body, we *are* a body!

To Do

The next time I'm sick, let me remember that it's through Your cross that all good things come to us. Not *around,* but *through.*

To Journal

Write about a time you experienced sickness. What did you learn from it? Did it make you more compassionate? Did you appreciate health more? Have you ever experienced God's physical healing?

Prayer

Dear Jesus, help me remember that now suffering isn't just a physical trial. You have filled it with spiritual meaning and redemptive efficacy!

August 31

Your body, too, will share in My glory. On the last day, your disembodied soul will receive your body back—as I did—a glorified body! Your best possible body, your best possible self!

God's Word

". . . [N]ot only the creation, but we ourselves . . . groan inwardly as we wait for . . . the redemption of our bodies" (Romans 8:23).

Words of Wisdom

Many Catholics struggle with the reality of the resurrection of the body, even though the Apostles' Creed states: "I believe in the resurrection of the body," which refers to Jesus's body *and* our bodies. Many Catholics also mistakenly believe they will be reincarnated, but there is no such thing as reincarnation! The human person is one: body and soul. You cannot be another body or another soul.

To do

Visit a cemetery and read the names of all the people you will meet in the flesh someday!

To journal

How can you strengthen your belief in the resurrection of the body? Write out how you would explain theology of the body to others in a nutshell. Rehearse.

Prayer

Dear Jesus, by making everything new, Your heaven is total healing of every kind: physical and spiritual. I am so comforted by this thought.

September 1

You are My co-creator. I have gifted you with autonomy and the ability and duty to work and create. Go for it! I trust you.

God's Word

". . . [F]ill the earth and subdue it; and have dominion over . . . every living thing that moves upon the earth" (Genesis 1:28).

Words of Wisdom

Work—of whatever kind—is an important dimension of human existence. We are called to govern the world in justice and holiness. Work praises God and reflects His creative love. Thank God for the gift of work (especially on Mondays).

To Do

Find ways to create and be creative even at rote, monotonous jobs. Remember that although working outside the home is a great thing, being a homemaker and raising the next generation is a very noble thing too.

To Journal

Work is meant to make life more human. How? If this has not been your experience, how can you change it?

Prayer

Dear Jesus, people often misunderstand Your command to "have dominion" over the earth. It means to care for the earth and use it with respect for the purpose of human advancement, not destroy it. We are responsible for this earth because it is Yours and ours. We are stewards.

September 2

Most of your life will be spent in some kind of work. Some will be drudgery; some will be life-giving, both to you and to others.

"In the sweat of your face you shall eat bread . . ." (Genesis 3:19).

Words of wisdom

"When I have to work at practicing patience in a particular relationship, I find it helpful to pray. 'I love you in the Heart of Christ which burns with love for you!' You can incorporate this prayer into your daily life as you rub shoulders with classmates, co-workers, and family members." (Sr. John Mary of the Indwelling Trinity, CP, www.passionistnuns.org)

To do

After original sin, all our relationships—with God, ourselves, each other, and all creation—became wounded. Jesus came to restore our relationships. How is God helping you to restore each of these relationships in your life?

To journal

Bl. James Alberione listed the importance of spiritual work in the following order: interior life, desires, prayer, good example, suffering, action. Which do you feel most drawn to?

Prayer

Dear Jesus, I want to "be noble, for I am made of stardust," and "humble, for I am made of earth." (Serbian proverb)

September 3

I have willed that you be intimately connected to the welfare and destiny of the earth. Environmental problems arise from lack of understanding of your vocation as caretaker!

God's Word

"A righteous man has regard for the life of his beast . . ." (Proverbs 12:10).

Words of Wisdom

Nature and its resources are the basis of our life: nutrition, development, health, energy, etc. Nature precedes and supports technology. Non-believers are scandalized by Christians who don't care for the earth. Cultivate an appreciation and reverence for nature.

To Do

Be a good steward of the earth. Search online for quick and easy ways to be green. What's your "always do" green list? Learn more about living in harmony with nature from Native Americans like Catholic Chief Black Elk. Read *Ten Commandments for the Environment: Pope Benedict XVI Speaks Out for Creation and Justice* by Woodeene Koenig-Bricker.

To Journal

Do you need to get back in touch with nature? Do you appreciate the entire natural world as a gift from God? Rate your stewardship of the earth on a scale of 1–10.

Prayer

Dear Jesus, we humans are the natural priests of creation. Only we can be grateful and offer everything back to You.

September 4

The foundation of all work is the mystery and gift of My creation. You didn't make any of the resources you harvest and fashion. All is gift.

God's word

". . . [W]hen he marked out the foundations of the earth, then I was beside him, like a master workman . . . rejoicing in his inhabited world and delighting in the sons of men" (Proverbs 8:29–31).

Words of wisdom

The Eastern Church never lost the cosmic sense of Jesus's lordship as king of the universe nor of God's beauty in nature, worship, and art.

To do

Go to an Eastern Rite (Byzantine, Chaldean, Maronite, Armenian, or Syro-Malabarese) Catholic Mass—called Divine Liturgy. Mark next year's calendar to celebrate Earth Day in the spring (as a believer)!

To journal

Saints and mystics were close to creation because they were close to the Creator. They saw every bush aflame. St. Francis loved brother sun, sister moon, and animals because he saw God's beauty in them. How do you see God's beauty in nature?

Prayer

Dear Jesus, humans who destroy creation and those who believe creation is more important than humans make the same mistake. They don't see man as *part* of nature, part of the solution. Open our eyes.

September 5

Through work you will help realize your humanity. What gives work its value and dignity is not the type of work, but the fact that it is you, a human person, doing the work!

God's Word

"The sabbath was made for man, not man for the sabbath" (Mark 2:27).

Words of wisdom

In the ancient world, manual labor was for slaves. It was judged unworthy of free people. Even today, manual labor is often looked down on. But man himself dignifies and humanizes all work. Man's work is not a commodity, it is the act of a person.

To do

The next time you see someone engaged in manual labor: garbage collection, landscaping, street cleaning, window-washing, etc., say hello and thank them for their service.

To journal

Are you engaged primarily in manual or intellectual work? Which do you prefer? Why? Write out your understanding of the meaning of work and what it means to you. Write about your experience of work so far. Do you feel valued as a person at work?

Prayer

Dear Jesus, let me be like the stonemason who, when asked what he was doing, didn't say, "I'm cutting stone." He said, "I'm building a cathedral."

September 6

Work serves your humanity and doesn't detract from it. It is not just for survival, but should enhance the whole human community and draw you closer together.

God's Word

". . . [M]an does not live by bread alone, but . . . by everything that proceeds out of the mouth of the LORD" (Deuteronomy 8:3).

Words of Wisdom

"There are no small parts, only small actors." This expression of Konstantin Stanislavsky, referring to the stage, can also be applied to work: "There are no small jobs. . . ." Check into lay movements such as Opus Dei (Work of God), that are about sanctifying time and ordinary things, as well as excellence in one's field of work for the glory of God and peace to men.

To Do

St. Thérèse of Lisieux and Mother Teresa urged us to do little things with great love. How can you put love into your work?

To Journal

Jesus looked at the rich young man in the Gospels with love. There must have been something in his demeanor that made this love visible. Describe what that might have been.

Prayer

Dear Jesus, "grant us the wisdom, virtue, and love that sustained You in Your toil-filled days" (Prayers of the Pauline Family).

September 7

I bless the world of work. I bless the worker. Work is meant to bless, not oppress. Employer and worker are in a totally interdependent relationship. You need one another. It can work out for both of you! There is enough for everyone.

God's Word

". . . [Y]ou shall give him his hire on the day he earns it . . . lest he cry against you to the LORD, and it be sin in you" (Deuteronomy 24:15).

Words of Wisdom

When work is misunderstood, humans are misunderstood. The problem is usually that the right order (people first, things second) has been reversed. In reality, good economics, economics that work, does put people first.

To do

Do the workers come first at your workplace? Even if your workplace is unfair, think of the people your work is serving, and do it for them.

To journal

There is also justice owed to the employer: punctuality, accuracy, good use of time, industriousness, effort, and honesty. How is this at your workplace? How are you at this?

Prayer

Dear Jesus, "see amid what fatigue, sufferings, and snares we live our hard days. See the physical and moral sufferings. Comfort us" (Prayers of the Pauline Family).

September 8

No one is the servant of the work—no matter how important the work is—work serves you and all humanity! People develop themselves through love of work.

God's Word

" . . . I command you, You shall open wide your hand to your brother, to the needy and to the poor . . ." (Deuteronomy 15:11).

Words of Wisdom

When the dignity of the human person is violated, poverty emerges. As a Church, we are called to "an option for the poor," that is, to see Christ in the "least of these," to better their conditions.

To Do

Some will feel called to help the poor by working for change on a large scale, others by doing individual acts of charity and meeting immediate needs. Which do you feel called to? Do you spend all your money on yourself or do you give some to charity?

To Journal

What plight of the poor most moves you? Why? How do you deal with greed in your life, with lust for more money, and desire for the latest fashions and gadgets?

Prayer

Dear Jesus, "inspire us with thoughts of faith, peace, moderation, and thrift, so that together with our daily bread, we will seek spiritual goods and heaven" (Prayers of the Pauline Family).

September 9

Man's ingenuity has found amazing ways to overcome difficulties in the world of work, especially regarding the safeguarding of human rights. But there is a long way to go to apply these in the developing world.

God's Word

"Open your mouth . . . for the rights of all who are left desolate" (Proverbs 31:8). "For the needy shall not always be forgotten, and the hope of the poor shall not perish for ever" (Psalm 9:18).

Words of Wisdom

Read the encyclicals of John Paul II *On Human Work* and *On Social Concern* to understand the Church's teaching on work (www.vatican.va).

To do

Educate yourself about local workers' movements and see what you can do to help.

To journal

Write what you know of the challenges and struggles your parents, grandparents, or great-grandparents had with work. You are part of a long chain, a heritage, of work!

Prayer

Dear Jesus, "inspire social laws which are in conformity with the Church's teaching. May charity and justice reign together through the sincere cooperation of all members of society" (Prayers of the Pauline Family).

September 10

The world is becoming more interconnected. Let this be an opportunity for mutual help, not exploitation.

God's word

". . . [T]he meek shall possess the land, and delight themselves in abundant prosperity" (Psalm 37:11).

Words of wisdom

Globalization has always been with us, but never like today! Globalization has its advantages and disadvantages. One of the biggest problems is that the highest possible price is being asked for goods that have been produced by workers paid the lowest possible wage.

To do

Grab a camera and spend one hour on a busy downtown street. Take pictures of as many "countries" as you can: people of different nationalities, foreign products, cars, foods, pets, clothes, etc. Watch *The Story of Stuff* or *Corporation* to learn about how globalized production and business works.

To journal

"Think globally, act locally." How often do you think about how your actions, especially your buying habits, affect people on the other side of the globe? You can't stop living and consuming, but what can you do to be a more responsible consumer?

Prayer

Dear Jesus, "deliver us from all exploiters who do not recognize the rights and dignity of the human person" (Prayers of the Pauline Family).

September 11

The development of technology is in harmony with My plan to develop people and their world. Technology is misused if it is used against man and not for man.

God's word

". . . I have filled him with the Spirit of God, with ability and intelligence, with knowledge and all craftsmanship . . ." (Exodus 31:3). "All these rely upon their hands, and each is skillful in his own work. Without them a city cannot be established . . ." (Sirach 38:31–32).

Words of wisdom

Contrary to popular belief, the Amish do not despise technology. They test it to see if it truly enhances their way of life, then adopt it or not. Test the technology in your life.

To do

Consecrate, or entrust the world of technology to God. Give your computer a saint's name or the name of a virtue.

To journal

Do you keep yourself firmly in charge of your technology or do you allow it to enslave you? How can you regain control? How can we insure that technology is used humanly?

Prayer

"Hail Mary, Mother, Teacher, and Queen of every work. Today we consecrate to you all our machines, undertakings, and the fatigue of daily work" (Prayers of the Pauline Family).

September 12

Humankind is changed by your developments, inventions, and ingenuity, but you are not changed in your essence.

God's Word

"The earth is the LORD's and the fullness thereof, the world and those who dwell therein . . ." (Psalm 24:1).

Words of Wisdom

Even though we've created machines that create machines and imitate human intelligence, we are still the ultimate creator of our own handiwork. Technology *can* take away personal creativity and employment. We can even program technology to harm us or eliminate us! But we can and must continue to master and take responsibility for our technology. We have intrinsic worth that no machine can be programmed to "decide" against.

To Do

Technology is not a "God-free" zone! Learn about business ethics and bio-ethics. Look for religious and moral references in *WIRED* magazine. Who is the patron saint of computer programmers? Why?

To Journal

Physicist and astronomer Aileen O'Donoghue finds God in cold steel (http://it.stlawu.edu/~aodo). Where and how do you find God in technology?

Prayer

Dear Jesus, "save us from those who deceitfully try to deprive us of the gift of faith and confidence in Your providence" (Prayers of the Pauline Family).

September 13

Although you may experience many burdens and trials in work, work is good. Learn to make peace with work.

God's word

". . . [H]old fast to your duty, busy yourself with it, grow old while doing your task" (Sirach 11:20 NAB).

Words of wisdom

Many successful workplaces emphasize the individual's talents as well as teamwork in a relaxed, playful, and creative atmosphere. The dignity of the worker seems to be upheld in these workplaces. What are some reasons that other less creative work atmospheres favor a robot-like worker? How can you humanize your workplace?

To do

Do you know your strengths, weaknesses, working style? Taking a work-aptitude test might help you discover what type of work is most suitable for you. Have you thought seriously about switching jobs? Changing fields? What's holding you back? Make a list of the pros and cons of making the move. Pray over it and then act.

To journal

What was the best job you ever had? Why? What would your dream job be? Describe in detail.

Prayer

Dear Jesus, "we present to You the needs of all who carry on intellectual, moral, or physical work" (Prayers of the Pauline Family).

September 14

Work is not an isolated, compartmentalized part of your life. It permeates everything you do. Even leisure has an element of work, doesn't it?

God's word

"I do it all for the sake of the gospel, that I may share in its blessings" (1 Corinthians 9:23).

Words of wisdom

Work is meant to build up the family, to teach what it means to be human, and to contribute to the common good. Assess your work in this bigger picture.

To do

Because so much work is done outside the home, we can forget that the home is the first school of work. With a video camera, shadow three different families to see how they juggle family and work inside and outside the home. Make them each a keepsake video.

To journal

We use the word "chore" to mean something tedious. But sometimes, is it just our attitude? What's a chore you find distasteful? Is it possible to change your attitude toward it?

Prayer

Good St. Joseph, assist all families in their many tasks. "You were the carpenter of Nazareth and work-teacher to the Son of God, who became a humble laborer for us" (Prayers of the Pauline Family).

September 15

The world of work and trade, and goods and services, has always brought My people together. Interconnectedness and interdependence is your reality and My plan!

God's Word

"The eye cannot say to the hand, 'I have no need of you . . .'" (1 Corinthians 12:21).

Words of Wisdom

We are always benefiting from the work of others, and from what is already given to us by the Creator. Although we may have worked hard for what we have, everything and everyone ultimately belongs to God. The common good includes the principle of common use, that is, even the right to private property is not absolute, because goods—beginning with the earth's resources—are meant for everyone. Indigenous peoples have always understood this.

To do

Volunteer for something outside of your comfort zone at work. See where it takes you! Try playing a computer game with gamers from around the world.

To journal

How have your horizons expanded through your work? Has your work involved travel? What wonderful people have you met through work?

Prayer

Dear Jesus, even though I grumble, I am grateful for my job and my ability to work.

September 16

The fact that there is hunger, unemployment, and underemployment means there is something wrong with the way the world of work has been organized and goods have been distributed.

God's Word

"He who supplies seed to the sower and bread for food will supply and multiply your resources and increase the harvest of your righteousness" (2 Corinthians 9:10).

Words of Wisdom

Human work cannot be seen only according to its economic purpose. Many people take drastic pay cuts for more meaningful work or to work for the Church. Any system that puts things or money before people and values can be labeled materialistic, whether it is capitalist or socialist.

To Do

Find your own way to contribute to the betterment of the world of work and support fellow workers and their families.

To Journal

Do you feel a sense of ownership of the work you do? How? Have you ever slipped into putting things or tasks before people? Were *you* ever put second to things or money? What happened?

Prayer

Dear Jesus, let us embrace a "social doctrine which assures the worker of a gradual social betterment and the kingdom of heaven" (Prayers of the Pauline Family).

September 17

Solidarity and community are natural among workers because all workers have the same basic needs and desires.

God's word

"Finally, all of you, have unity of spirit, sympathy, love of the brethren, a tender heart and a humble mind" (1 Peter 3:8).

Words of wisdom

Laws and standards in the workplace are necessary for everyone's protection, but we are still human beings, the human family, underneath it all. And if we are Christians, we are joined in the one body of Christ! Does being professional sometimes detract from your humanity and that of others? People become clients, vendors, or patients. Perhaps all that's needed is to maintain the inner awareness of the dignity of each individual and act accordingly.

To do

Try to resolve your working relationship with the most difficult person at your job.

To journal

How is your relationship with your employer? Your company? Your co-workers? Those you serve?

Prayer

Dear Jesus, may everyone be able to exercise their most basic right to work: to give one's gifts, to provide for oneself and one's family, and to contribute to society.

September 18

Even if you were completely incapacitated and incapable of work, your identity and your worth would still be completely intact.

God's word

". . . [D]o not be haughty, but associate with the lowly; never be conceited" (Romans 12:16). "Open your mouth, judge righteously, maintain the rights of the poor and needy" (Proverbs 31:9).

Words of Wisdom

In our competitive society, it is easy to equate our worth with our work, and to get our sense of identity solely from our job description. Whether we are doing well or not so well in the work world, remember: it is only one dimension of life.

To do

Unemployment (or insufficient wages) can be a serious matter, especially with a family to support. Few things can cause more stress or despair. Volunteer to teach literacy or computer skills to help others advance. Volunteer to do respite care for working families with needy children or elderly family members.

To journal

Have you ever been unemployed? Fired? Replaced? Demoted? Passed over for a promotion? Stuck in a dead-end job? How did it make you feel? How did you get over it?

Prayer

Dear Jesus, repeat the cry of Your heart: "I have compassion for the crowd" (Matthew 15:32).

September 19

Few people are doing exactly what they want at work or in life! It is up to you to find the supernatural in the natural. Even at your job.

God's Word

". . . God loves a cheerful giver" (2 Corinthians 9:7).

Words of Wisdom

Are you finding some kind of fulfillment at your work? Or is it just "what pays the bills"? Sometimes a sense of humor helps break the tension of work. Can you relate to work-place sitcoms?

To do

Resolve to make the necessary changes or stop complaining interiorly about what's lacking at your present job. Concentrate on making the proverbial "lemonade," and making things better for your co-workers.

To journal

Do you have a fulfilling job? Count your blessings! If you don't, how has the lack of fulfillment stretched you and made you seek it elsewhere? What skills or hidden talents have you discovered at work (that might not even be part of your job description)? What are experiences you've had at work that you'd never have had otherwise?

Prayer

Good St. Joseph, help us imitate your work ethic. "With Mary you shared sufferings and joys, virtue, work, and union of mind and of heart" (Prayers of the Pauline Family).

September 20

What is progress? Progress means that work should continuously improve the lives of all, not just the few. The human family should advance together as much as possible.

God's Word

". . . [P]rosper for us the work of our hands" (Psalm 90:17 NRSV).

Words of Wisdom

Humans should *be* more because of their work, not just *have* more. Work that achieves greater justice and better relationships is more important than technical advances. Technical advances can supply the material for true human progress, but can't actually make it happen. We need the will to make progress benefit everyone.

To do

Vote for family-friendly legislation that allows for a family wage, that is, for one parent to stay home and care for children; allowances for stay-at-home or single parents; daycare in the workplace; extended maternity and paternity leaves; and assistance and remuneration for those taking care of elderly family members.

To journal

How does your specific work—even in small ways—contribute to true progress?

Prayer

Dear Jesus, all of us—even single people—are really working for the family, because we are all working for the future, and children are the future! Thank You for this privilege.

September 21

Woman must be able to fulfill her own nature in the world of work. True progress means that women can take their rightful place in the family and society.

God's Word

"She girds her loins with strength and makes her arms strong. She perceives that her merchandise is profitable. Her lamp does not go out at night" (Proverbs 31:17–18).

Words of Wisdom

Work should enhance family life because the future of society depends on the nurturing of children. Every mother is a working mother. Mothers who also work outside the home need support, as do those who return to work after raising their families.

To Do

Watch *North Country* about the harassment of women on the job. Have you ever experienced this? What did you do or are you doing about it?

To Journal

We have proven that we can "be men" in the workplace. But can we be women? Femininity in the workplace hasn't been tried and found wanting, it just hasn't been tried. Do you agree? Comment.

Prayer

Dear Jesus, may we women bring our influence and perspective to the world of work inside and outside the home, and receive due recognition and recompense for our work.

September 22

Let me be the Lord of your work! Give me a place at your workbench, whatever that might be.

God's Word

"[A]nd you shall love the Lord your God with all your heart, and with all your soul, and with all your mind, and with all your strength" (Mark 12:30).

Words of Wisdom

Work occupies so much of our time, energy, thoughts, and life-blood, that we need a "spirituality of work." In a sense we work out our salvation at our work! Work should bring us closer to God.

To do

How is your work in the "image of God?" Transform the way you look at the littlest, most mundane tasks that you find hard to relate to God.

To journal

We share in Jesus Christ's threefold mission—priest, prophet, and king—by our Baptism. How do you (as priest) offer your work back to God? How do you (as prophet) live the Gospel at work? How do you (as king) make the world a more just place through your work?

Prayer

Dear Jesus, as Christians we should be even more motivated to share in your creative, redeeming, and sanctifying work for the good of all. Enflame my heart with love for You and for people.

September 23

On the seventh day, I rested from the work of creation. The seventh day is My gift to you and a foretaste of heaven.

God's word
"I was glad when they said to me, 'Let us go to the house of the LORD!'" (Psalm 122:1).

Words of wisdom
Why do we worship on Sunday and not Saturday? The Apostles celebrated the Eucharist on Sunday because Jesus rose on the seventh day of the week. It's a day to rest from work, shopping, etc., and to open our spirits to God, the transcendent, eternity, our ultimate end.

To do
Ask your Jewish friends about their celebration of the Sabbath as the day of rest and renewal. Read *Dies Domini: On Keeping the Lord's Day Holy* by John Paul II, and Wayne Muller's books on the Sabbath.

To journal
How do you use Sunday for your spiritual renewal (besides Mass)? If you work on Sunday, do you take another "sabbath day" for yourself? Write a "sabbath plan" (e.g.: sleep in, do a rosary walk, visit sick relatives/friends, enjoy nature, pray Vespers, read, etc.).

Prayer
Dear Jesus, help me to make my Sundays special, and orient my whole day to praising You!

September 24

I chose to be a worker. I chose manual labor like My earthly father, St. Joseph.

God's Word

"Is not this the carpenter's son?" (Matthew 13:55)

Words of Wisdom

By devoting most of his life to hidden physical labor, Jesus preached the Gospel of work—what's important is not the type of work but the person doing the work. "The primary basis of the value of work is man himself," says John Paul II (*On Human Work*, no. 6). We work in imitation of God who didn't just create the world and step back. God *sustains* the world.

To do

What is your workbench? Do you love it? Do you give it your all? When you pray the "Our Father," pray it for the entire working world that labors for its daily bread. Listen to Michael Card's "Joseph's Song."

To journal

Have you seen the bumper sticker: "My boss is a Jewish carpenter"? Besides actually being a carpenter, Jesus chose other images of work to describe Himself such as shepherd and vinedresser. Which one most appeals to you? Why?

Prayer

Dear Jesus, Divine Laborer and Friend of workers, look kindly on the working world and move us with Your grace from within.

September 25

My prophets, My apostles, and My friends were also workers. Let Me into your life of work.

God's Word

". . . [B]ecause he was of the same trade he [Paul] stayed with them, and they worked, for by trade they were tentmakers" (Acts 18:3).

Words of wisdom

Sports are a form of work. St. Paul used athletic imagery: "run so as to win," "I have finished the race, I have fought the good fight" (cf. 1 Corinthians 9:24, 2 Timothy 4:7). Offer your sports to God! Look to athletic role models like Bl. Pier Giorgio Frassati (skiing), Pope Pius XI (world-class mountain climber), Kim Yu-Na (gold medalist figure skater).

To do

Intellectual "white collar" work requires concentration of the mind. Manual jobs might lend themselves to more contemplation. Is there a balance of mental and physical work in your job? If not, what can you do to balance that when not at work?

To journal

St. Paul urges us not to be idle, but to work. Do you tend more toward laziness or workaholism? How can you improve your work ethic to avoid both?

Prayer

Dear Jesus, Your "yoke is easy" and Your "burden is light" (Matthew 11:30). Help me to work with love.

September 26

You will draw positive and negative attention at work because you are My follower. Without even trying, you will be a sign of hope to those who are searching, and a sign of contradiction to those who want to justify themselves.

God's Word

"... [Y]ou shall be my witnesses ... to the end of the earth" (Acts 1:8).

Words of Wisdom

It takes a lot to be true to yourself and take a stand for what's right at the very job that feeds you! But this is your real world, the arena where you really live and interact with others. You may want to pick your battles, but it's hard not to get embroiled in controversies at work once in a while. Being rigidly over-principled and loosely unprincipled are both unhelpful.

To do

Listen to Tom Booth's "Fragrance Song." How can you be the "fragrance of Christ" at work? (cf. 2 Corinthians 2:14)

To journal

How do you deal with challenges at work: temptations to compromise or hide your beliefs, gossip, religious or sexual harassment, unethical business practices or policies, intimidation, or unbridled ambition?

Prayer

Dear Jesus, my main field of apostolate as a lay Catholic is my place of work. Help me to be Your witness.

September 27

Don't forget that study is work, too. Whether or not you like to study, it is an important part of life.

God's Word

". . . [D]o not hide your wisdom. For wisdom is known through speech, and education through the words of the tongue" (Sirach 4:23–24).

Words of Wisdom

Some of the *Church's* greatest thinkers were also the *world's* greatest thinkers: St. Thomas Aquinas, St. Edith Stein, Bl. John Paul the Great. Check out these priest-scientists: Le Maître ("the Big Bang"), Copernicus (astronomy), Angelo Secci (astrophysics), and Brother Gregor Mendel (father of genetics). Check out Christian lay scientists Blaise Pascal (mathematician, inventor, physicist), Louis Pasteur (chemist, biologist), and Francis Collins (genetics).

To Do

Look up the patron saint of your particular work. Who would you nominate as a "living saint" in your line of work? Are you looking for a job? St. Cajetan is the patron of job seekers. Your work doesn't have a patron? What about you?

To Journal

Bl. James Alberione said, "Make everything the subject of meditation," that is, learn from everything. Journal about one small life lesson every day, starting today.

Prayer

Dear Jesus, may all the arts, sciences, and humanities sing Your praises!

September 28

I am the poor and neglected. If you want to know Me, if you want to be close to Me, look into the face of My poor.

God's word

". . . [A]s you did it to one of the least of these my brethren, you did it to me" (Matthew 25:40).

Words of wisdom

Before we can help the poor, we have to see them. Research the various types of poor and what can be done to help them. A new kind of poverty today is that of those poor in technology and media. Review the corporal and spiritual works of mercy.

To do

Each of us is only one person, and the needs of the world can be overwhelming. You probably already feel called toward something: building houses, mission trips, pro-life work, etc. Donate the amateur or professional skills you already have.

To journal

St. Lawrence, before he was martyred, was told to turn over the Church's treasure. He led his persecutors to the poor of Rome. How have the poor been a treasure for you?

Prayer

Dear Jesus, You said "I thirst." Let me do what I can to slake Your thirst as You appear in the distressing disguise of the poor.

September 29

What a privilege it is to serve! The day will come when you are too sick or old to work and serve, and others will be serving you. Only then will you realize that working and serving is not a duty, but a joy.

God's Word

"We must work the works of him who sent me, while it is day; night comes, when no one can work" (John 9:4).

Words of Wisdom

"How often we give ourselves to those around us and are disappointed in their response. You will never be disappointed in Jesus's response to the love and care you give to others." (Sr. Susan Louise Eder, OSFS, www.oblatesisters.org)

To Do

Do you have a permanent volunteer job? Why not choose one you know is doable and commit to it. In that way good intentions and lack of time won't get in the way.

To Journal

Write about your volunteer high points and low points. How can you improve your volunteer experiences?

Prayer

Dear Jesus, "if there is any kindness that I can show, let me do it now, for I shall not pass this way again." (Stephen Grellet)

September 30

After My life of manual work came My spiritual work of preaching and healing. Then I entered the next stage, My paschal mystery.

God's word

"When a woman is in travail she has sorrow, because her hour has come; but when she is delivered of the child, she no longer remembers the anguish, for joy that a child is born into the world" (John 16:21).

Words of wisdom

The nature of work is toil. An honest day's work, planning and building for the future, being of service, is good toil. Work was ordained from the beginning, even before the Fall.

To do

Everyone is invited to participate in Jesus's saving work by adding their own daily toil to His. Make a daily offering of your work to Jesus through Mary every day.

To journal

The paschal mystery constantly plays out its pattern in our lives in big and little ways. How have you been able to recognize Jesus's suffering, death, and resurrection in your life?

Prayer

Dear Jesus, "grant that my death may be serene. May my judgment be the moment in which the hard-working laborer joyfully receives the reward" (Prayers of the Pauline Family).

October 1

I chose to be born of a woman.

God's Word

". . . [W]hy is this granted me, that the mother of my Lord should come to me?" (Luke 1:43)

Words of Wisdom

There are four Marian dogmas (dogmas are solemnly defined truths of faith to be believed by all Catholics): Mary's Motherhood, Perpetual Virginity, Immaculate Conception, Assumption. We are already consecrated to God at our Baptism, and it is He that consecrates or makes holy, but Mary wants to help us lead a life of holiness—so we should let her! God's plan for the world is a family affair—and Mary is the mother of Jesus, the head, and His body, the Church. If Jesus is truly God, then Mary is truly the Mother of God. She cannot be mother of His human nature only, because Jesus is *one* divine Person. This does not make her divine. She is human.

To Do

We follow God's ways. Mary is God's way. If you aren't already consecrated or entrusted to Mary, read St. Louis de Montfort's books and make a consecration.

To Journal

What's your relationship with Mary like?

Prayer

Holy Mother of God, pray for us!

October 2

My Mother is the only woman who will ever be simultaneously both virgin and mother.

God's Word

"The virgin will conceive and give birth to a son, and will call him Immanuel" (Isaiah 7:14 NIV).

Words of Wisdom

The dogma of Mary's Perpetual Virginity states that Mary was a virgin before, during, and after Jesus's conception and birth. Jesus's was not only a miraculous conception, but a miraculous birth (cf. *Fundamentals of Catholic Dogma* by Ludwig Ott, and *The Mystery of Mary* by Fr. Paul Haffner).

To do

At Vatican II, some Council Fathers wanted a document on Mary, but they decided she is so intrinsically linked to the Church that they devoted chapter eight of the *Dogmatic Constitution on the Church* to her instead. Pray the Litany of the Blessed Virgin to which Pope Paul VI added *Mater Ecclesiae* (Mother of the Church).

To journal

When John Paul II was shot, he looked around St. Peter's Square for a Madonna, but found none! When he recovered, he had an image of *Mater Ecclesiae* installed, overlooking the square. Reflect on Mary's role in your life. Does she need a bigger part?

Prayer

Mother of the Church, pray for us!

October 3

My Mother was preserved at her conception from original sin in view of My redemption.

God's Word

"I will put enmity between you and the woman, and between your seed and her seed; he shall bruise your head, and you shall bruise his heel" (Genesis 3:15).

Words of Wisdom

"Pledge your life to something great. Aim high with your ideal because nothing is impossible with God! On October 3, at age 18, I offered my life to our Immaculata at the Schoenstatt Shrine in Sleepy Eye, Minnesota, to work for pure and intact family life in America." (Sr. M. Jessica Swedzinski, ISSM)

To do

Watch *The Song of Bernadette*—Golden Globe Best Picture of 1943. Read *Bernadette Speaks* by Fr. René Laurentin. Research the continual miracles at Lourdes connected to the healing spring of water Our Lady had Bernadette uncover there.

To journal

St. Bernadette was asthmatic and sickly, but strong in spirit and love for her family, God, and the Blessed Mother. What are your physical weaknesses? How do you work with them? From where do you draw your inner strength?

Prayer

Queen conceived without original sin, pray for us!

October 4

My Mother was assumed, body and soul, into heavenly glory. The only human body in heaven besides My own, is a female body. Where we have gone, you will follow. I am going to prepare a place for you.

God's Word

". . . [A] woman clothed with the sun, with the moon under her feet, and on her head a crown of twelve stars" (Revelation 12:1).

Words of Wisdom

Mary's assumption and coronation were really one event! As soon as Mary arrived in heaven, she became the queen of it! Make Mary the queen of your life.

To Do

Learn about the amazing story of Our Lady of Guadalupe. Virtually overnight, she converted eight million Mexican natives to the faith by appearing as a pregnant Indian virgin with the moon under her feet. She is patroness of the preborn because she stopped Aztec human sacrifice. Get involved in the pro-life movement: www.rockforlife.org, www.humanlife.org, www.hli.org, www.40 daysforlife.com.

Watch *Our Lady of Guadalupe: Mother of Hope!* by Dan Lynch.

To Journal

Write out your favorite hymn to Our Lady, or write her a poem.

Prayer

Queen assumed into heaven, pray for us!

October 5

I will that My Mother be honored. The best way to honor her is to imitate her. She was My first and best disciple.

God's Word

". . . [A]ll generations will call me blessed . . ." (Luke 1:48).

Words of Wisdom

The name for the special honor shown Mary is hyperdulia. If one were to adore Mary it would be idolatry or Mariolatry. To understand proper devotion to Mary, read Paul VI's *Marialis Cultus*, and the *Catechism of the Catholic Church* (nos. 963–975).

To do

Wear a blessed miraculous medal (they come in all sizes, for watches, as necklaces, etc.). How about attaching it to a backpack or purse? What is the prayer around the edge of the medal? What is the symbolism on the back of the medal? Medals are not amulets, good luck charms, or magic. They are sacramentals. Read *Catherine Labouré: Visionary of the Miraculous Medal* by Fr. René Laurentin.

To journal

God doesn't outfit people for a mission then cast them aside. Mary continues her mission as Mother of God and the Church from heaven. What mission is God outfitting you for? What is something you would want to keep doing in heaven?

Prayer

Virgin most renowned, pray for us!

October 6

I channel power and grace through My most holy Mother. Entrust yourself to her.

God's Word

". . . [H]e who is mighty has done great things for me . . ." (Luke 1:49).

Words of Wisdom

Bl. John Paul II carried a chemical-stained copy of *True Devotion to the Blessed Virgin Mary* by St. Louis de Montfort when he worked in the mines. His papal motto was *Totus Tuus* (All Yours)—a shortened form of the consecration prayer: "I am all Yours and all that I possess I offer to You, my loveable Jesus, through Mary, Your most holy Mother." Carry something to remind you of Jesus and Mary.

To do

Our Lady of Czestochowa (Poland) is a Black Madonna (black in color from age). The Black Madonnas (found all over the world) tend to be of mysterious origins. Learn about the yearly walking pilgrimage to Jasna Gora where the image of Our Lady of Czestochowa is kept. Organize a walking pilgrimage to a local Marian shrine! Learn about St. Maximilian Kolbe and the Militia of the Immaculata—is there a branch near you?

To journal

What does consecrating or entrusting yourself to Mary mean to you?

Prayer

Virgin most powerful, pray for us!

October 7

My Mother has many gifts to give you. The Rosary—a Gospel prayer—is one of her greatest gifts.

God's word

"My soul magnifies the Lord . . ." (Luke 1:46).

Words of wisdom

Today is the feast of Our Lady of the Rosary. It was originally instituted in 1572 as the feast of Our Lady of Victory, because of the victory of the European naval fleet over the invading Turks at the Battle of Lepanto. Make the Rosary a consistent part of your life.

To do

Have you memorized how to say the Rosary so that you can lead it? Do you know which days to say which mysteries? Research the history of the Rosary. What is St. Dominic's connection to the Rosary? Join the Confraternity of the Rosary. Use Rosary meditation books to help you go deeper. Use a Rosary CD, DVD, or app, www.downloadsforcatholics.com.

To journal

Which are your favorite mysteries of the Rosary: joyful, sorrowful, luminous, or glorious? Why? What is the Rosary of your life (the major God-events of your life)?

Prayer

Queen of the most holy Rosary, pray for us!

October 8

My Mother was poor. She understands and cares about the travails of the poor.

God's word

"He has put down the mighty from their thrones, and exalted those of low degree . . ." (Luke 1:52).

Words of wisdom

"Throughout the day, strive to 'live Jesus' in a spirit of profound humility toward God and a great gentleness toward neighbor. This enables us to acknowledge our own poverty, the need to depend on God for all things, and ultimately reverence each poor person as the holy temple of God." (Sr. Joy Katharine Brown, VHM, www.toledovisitation.org)

To do

Mary was among the poor. How are you mindful of the poor in your life? Is there some particular thing you do for the poor? Consider sponsoring a child or family; volunteering at a soup kitchen or food pantry; taking time to talk with homeless people, learn their names, and listen to their stories; teaching adult literacy; and supporting legislation that will better the lives of the poor. Do you live simply so that others might simply live?

To journal

One of the Beatitudes is "Blessed are the poor in spirit" (Matthew 5:3). What does this mean to you?

Prayer

Mirror of justice, pray for us!

October 9

My Mother goes where there is tragedy, violence, and human struggle. She warns, encourages, pleads, teaches, and comforts.

God's word

"Let it be to me according to your word" (Luke 1:38).

Words of wisdom

Before the Rwandan genocide in 1991, Our Lady appeared in Kibeho, Rwanda, warning people of what was to come. She identified herself as "The Mother of the Word." Her last words were words of love, asking people to heed her messages even in the future. Heed Mary's voice in your life.

To do

Read genocide survivor Immaculée Ilibagiza's story *Left to Tell*, or watch *The Diary of Immaculée* on DVD. Immaculée hid with other women in a tiny bathroom for weeks. Learn how her faith grew strong under these horrific conditions.

To journal

The Rwandan nightmare didn't come out of nowhere. Unnatural situations of favoring one tribe over another were created by European colonists. Hate radio went unchecked as it escalated for years. As in all wars, enemies were dehumanized. What are your prejudices? Is there a group of people you disdain? Do you believe that nothing like that could happen in your country? Rwanda is over 60 percent Catholic.

Prayer

Seat of wisdom, pray for us!

October 10

A sign of the presence of My Holy Spirit is joy. The Holy Spirit over-shadowed My Mother, so she lives in profound joy and brings joy wherever she goes.

God's Word

". . . [M]y spirit rejoices in God my Saviour" (Luke 1:47).

Words of Wisdom

"Ask the Holy Spirit to help you be that person God wants you to be—because nothing else matters! From this deep relationship with God, serenity and joy come automatically. Do not be afraid to ask for the gift of joy! It is there for the taking!" (Sr. Anne Breen, PDDM, www.pddm.us)

To do

Those who laugh at you today may pray with you tomorrow, unless you keep your light hidden. Let others share your joy! Find the poem "When Our Lady Returns to Walsingham." Learn about Our Lady of Walsingham. Who dethroned her? Why? Is she finally returning? Learn, meditate, and pray the Seven Joys of Mary.

To journal

Do you live in joy? Why or why not? Is your joy apparent to others? How do you express joy: quietly or exuberantly?

Prayer

Cause of our joy, pray for us!

October 11

My Mother has many ways of communicating with you.

God's Word

"For while gentle silence enveloped all things, and night in its swift course was now half gone, your all-powerful word leaped from heaven, from the royal throne, into the midst of the land that was doomed . . ." (Wisdom 18:14–15 NRSV).

Words of Wisdom

As great as language and noise are, sometimes we have experiences in life that take us beyond words, and teach us the value of silence. Our Lady of Knock (Ireland) appeared as a kind of tableau, completely silent. She communicated in silence.

To do

Many religious congregations have a period of grand silence at the beginning and end of the day in order to recollect themselves, examine their day, and pray. Set aside periods of silence for yourself: daily, weekly, and monthly. Watch *Into Great Silence*, about Carthusian monks who live in prayerful silence.

To journal

Do I embrace silence or avoid it? Is it a positive or negative experience for me? What comes up when I'm alone and silent? Do I need to get help for some of the negative things or memories that come up?

Prayer

Singular vessel of devotion, pray for us!

October 12

My Mother is the citizen of every country! She comes to you as one of you.

God's word

"I will lift up my hand to the nations . . . and they shall bring your sons in their bosom, and your daughters shall be carried on their shoulders" (Isaiah 49:22).

Words of wisdom

"Throughout history, from the greatest to the least, people have had recourse to Mary the Mother of God. Pope John Paul II took Mary as his mother after the death of his own mother. With Mary's protection, my family escaped the Vietnamese communist regime. Even football players and fans have used terms such as 'the immaculate reception' and 'Hail Mary pass.' My advice is to call on Mary daily!" (Sr. Gioan Linh Nguyen, FSP, www.daughtersofstpaul.org)

To do

Learn about Our Lady of La Vang (Vietnam) who appeared with two angels to persecuted Catholics in the jungle. What does "la vang" mean? Learn about Vietnamese culture. Watch the film *Green Dragon* about Vietnamese refugees in the United States. Pray the "Little Office of the Blessed Virgin Mary."

To journal

Which devotion, title, or apparition of Mary most appeals to you? Why?

Prayer

Queen of patriarchs, pray for us!

October 13

Although My Mother is now the citizen of every country, her original homeland was the Holy Land.

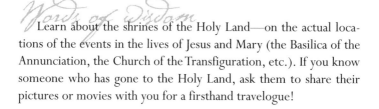

"...Abraham shall become a great and mighty nation, and all the nations of the earth shall bless themselves by him" (Genesis 18:18). "Blessed be the Lord God of Israel, for he has visited and redeemed his people ..." (Luke 1:68).

Learn about the shrines of the Holy Land—on the actual locations of the events in the lives of Jesus and Mary (the Basilica of the Annunciation, the Church of the Transfiguration, etc.). If you know someone who has gone to the Holy Land, ask them to share their pictures or movies with you for a firsthand travelogue!

Pray for the peace of Jerusalem, for an end to the Middle East crises, and for the Christians of the Middle East—descendants of the first Christians. Pray for the Catholic-Jewish dialogue.

Mary was a Jewish maiden of the tribe of Judah. How do you think Mary felt about her people? How do you feel about your people?

Tower of David, pray for us!

October 14

My Mother's heart is as big as the world. She holds you all in her heart.

God's Word

"... [T]hat thoughts out of many hearts may be revealed" (Luke 2:35).

Words of Wisdom

Did you know that Pope John Paul II was shot in St. Peter's Square on May 13—the Feast of Our Lady of Fatima—and the bullet is now in Our Lady of Fatima's crown in Portugal? Life is always richer, fuller, sweeter, and more amazing with Our Lady.

To do

Learn about Our Lady of Fatima (Portugal). Watch *The Miracle of Our Lady of Fatima*. Read *In Lucia's Own Words*. (Lucia Santos and her cousins, Francisco and Jacinta were the seers.) Join the World Apostolate of Fatima. What did Our Lady of Fatima say about World War I and World War II? When did Pope John Paul II consecrate the world to the Immaculate Heart of Mary as she had asked at Fatima? What was the "Third Secret of Fatima"?

To journal

Jacinta, only seven years old when Our Lady of Fatima first appeared, took Our Lady's message to heart. What would you do if Our Lady appeared to you?

Prayer

House of gold, pray for us!

October 15

My Mother adapts herself to everyone. In her apparitions and through devotions to her, she emanates the warmth of the Gospel from within various cultures.

God's Word

"Behold, your mother!" (John 19:27)

Words of Wisdom

"Nothing compares to the comfort of a mother's arms! Whether they are my own mother's or my heavenly Mother's, they mean welcome, comfort, and peace. Thank Mary for modeling a mother's heart for all women." (Sr. M. Jean Louise Schafer, OSF, www.dillingen franciscansusa.org)

To Do

The Ark of the Covenant contained the tablets of the Ten Commandments, the rod of Aaron, and manna. Mary, the new Ark of the Covenant, contained the living Word of God. Italian culture is full of an appreciation of beauty. Learn about these Madonnas in particular: Our Lady of the Streets, Our Lady of Loreto, Our Lady of Pompei, Our Lady of Good Counsel, Our Lady of Tears. Learn about the Marian piety of the Italian saint Alphonsus de Liguori.

To Journal

What is your favorite painting, portrayal, or icon of Mary? If you had to paint a Madonna, what would she look like? Would she have Jesus with her?

Prayer

Ark of the covenant, pray for us!

October 16

My Mother was foretold and prefigured from the beginning of salvation history.

God's word

"A garden locked is my sister, my bride, a garden locked, a fountain sealed" (Song of Songs 4:12).

Words of wisdom

"Beseech Mary to teach you the art and beauty of silence, for none had greater interior silence and recollection than she. It was in silence that Elijah experienced God's presence in the tiny whisper. It was in silence that Mary worked at Nazareth, contemplating her beautiful Son and sovereign Lord. In silence we allow God to speak most intimately to our hearts and draw us nearer to Him." (Sr. Mary Michael Reiss, Carmel, DCJ, www.carmelitedcj.org)

To do

Enroll in the Confraternity of Our Lady of Mount Carmel if you haven't already, and wear the brown scapular or scapular medal. Learn about St. Simon Stock to whom Our Lady of Mount Carmel gave the scapular. Place fresh flowers before an image of Our Lady at church or at home whenever you can.

To journal

Mountains are places of God's revelation. What are your mountains?

Prayer

Gate of heaven, pray for us!

October 17

Everything can be the subject of meditation and prayer for those who have eyes to see.

God's word
"But Mary kept all these things, pondering them in her heart" (Luke 2:19).

Words of wisdom
Our Lady of Pontmain, known as "Our Lady of Hope," or "Our Lady of Prayer," is an incredible apparition that teaches the importance of prayer. She saved a district from the ravages of war. Only children could see her. When a baby reached out her arms to her, Mary smiled and laughed.

To do
Mary, above all, was a woman of prayer. Pray the Liturgy of the Hours. The Liturgy of the Hours is basically praying the psalms. Mary prayed the psalms—you'll be praying them with her! Check out www.ebreviary.com/ or www.downloadsforcatholics.com. Search for "breviary" on your phone's app store.

To journal
Most of us have to be contemplatives-in-action. Are you a contemplative, prayerful person, or are you becoming so? Contemplation should make us persons of hope because in contemplation we will see things from God's perspective. How can you be a person of more hope?

Prayer
Morning star, pray for us!

October 18

I will my healing power to flow through my Mother.

God's Word

"Behold, I am the handmaid of the Lord" (Luke 1:38).

Words of Wisdom

Women can be notorious for not taking care of their own health or downplaying illnesses. Take care of your health, go to doctors, take medicine, but also pray for good health.

To do

Our Lady of Good Health of Vailankanni appears beautifully attired and holding a baby boy. She asks for a cup of milk for her child. In return, people are cured. Learn about Our Lady of Aparecida. What do people leave at her shrine in thanksgiving for restoration of good health? Wear something blue during the months of May and October in honor of Our Lady. Read St. Bernard's Marian writings.

To journal

How is your health physically spiritually, psychologically, and emotionally? Do you take care of your health? Remember, the best medicine is prevention. Do you get enough sleep? Overeat? Under-eat? Exercise? Our physical and spiritual well-being—mind-body connection—are totally interrelated. Do you ask for and trust in God's healing at all levels? Write out your health inventory.

Prayer

Health of the sick, pray for us!

October 19

My Mother shared in My passion with her own passion.

God's Word ". . . [A]nd a sword will pierce through your own soul also . . ." (Luke 2:35).

Words of Wisdom Melanie Mathieu-Calvet and Maxim Giraud were the young seers of Our Lady of La Salette. Maxim was what we call hyperactive today. He even threw a stone at Our Lady to see if she was real, and Melanie was always reprimanding him. Melanie and Maxim's lives were poor and difficult and only became more difficult after the apparitions. But Maxim was always cheerful and willing to tell the story of Our Lady over and over to the point of exhaustion. Their story is a very human one of struggle, and of how even chosen visionaries can be affected by others' lack of faith and human compassion.

To do Learn about Our Lady of La Salette who appeared sitting, head in hands, weeping. What sins of humanity was she weeping over? Learn, meditate, and pray the Seven Sorrows of Mary.

To journal What is your passion (in the sense of Our Lord's passion or suffering)? Compassion means "to suffer with." Who do you suffer with?

Prayer Refuge of sinners, pray for us!

October 20

My Mother has many children. There is no such thing as an orphan.

God's Word

". . . [T]he mother of Jesus said to him, 'They have no wine'" (John 2:3). "The LORD . . . saves the crushed in spirit" (Psalm 34:18).

Words of Wisdom

The former USSR is recovering from an atheistic regime. Religion was almost completely eradicated and the spirit of the people crushed. Many houses of worship were destroyed, but Our Lady never left her people. Mary will stay with you when your spirit is crushed.

To Do

Eastern Europe has a beautiful tradition of icons that it received from the ancient Eastern Christians. Learn about icons (and the discipline under which they are created), especially Our Lady of Kazan—returned to the Russian Orthodox Church by John Paul II. Learn about the *Theotokos* (Mother of God) icons thought to be painted by St. Luke. Learn about the rebirth of the Catholic Church in Russia and how you can help by visiting www.vladmission.org.

To Journal

Pray with an icon of Our Lady and write your reflections. (If you don't have an icon or picture of an icon, use some other image of Mary.)

Prayer

Comforter of the afflicted, pray for us!

October 21

My Mother involves herself in the historical struggles of nations and peoples.

God's Word

"When the Most High gave to the nations their inheritance . . . he fixed the bounds of the peoples . . ." (Deuteronomy 32:8).

Words of Wisdom

Marian apparitions and interventions are not just history, they are ongoing. Whenever people invoke her help, she doesn't fail. The peaceful "People Power" revolution in the Philippines, 1986, was accomplished with the Rosary. Honor Mary in a special way on her day, Saturday, especially by going to Mass if you can. Do the "Five First Saturdays." Join the Legion of Mary or another Marian organization. Learn about the Legion of Mary's Frank Duff and Edel Quinn (both from Ireland).

To Do

Excellent books to put on your reading list are: *The Reed of God* by Caryll Houselander, *Mary, in Her Own Words* by Fr. Gary Caster, *John Paul II: A Marian Treasury*, *Those Who Saw Her* by Catherine Odell, and *The Other Faces of Mary* by Ann Ball.

To Journal

What are your earliest recollections of Mary? Write out your history with Mary from as far back as you can remember until now.

Prayer

Help of Christians, pray for us!

October 22

My Mother is spoken of throughout My word, sometimes explicitly, sometimes implicitly. Search the Scriptures and you will find her.

God's word

"He has shown strength with his arm, he has scattered the proud in the imagination of their hearts" (Luke 1:51).

Words of wisdom

The Scriptures are filled with types of Mary. Types, or typology, relate Old Testament persons and objects to those of the New Testament. The Old Testament has validity in itself, but it also has layers. In God's ways we see patterns. For example, think about Mary as the "new Eve." (Many Old Testament women prefigure Mary.)

To do

Heresies and misunderstandings about Mary imply heresies and misunderstandings about Jesus. Read Scott Hahn's *Hail Holy Queen*, and *Queen Mother* by Edward Sri, to see how Catholic devotion to Mary is biblical. Read *A Protestant Pastor Looks at Mary* by Charles Dickson. Learn about Our Lady of Altotting and Our Lady of Kevelaer.

To journal

What can you share with others about what Mary has done for you and means to you? How can you explain Mary to your non-Catholic, Christian friends?

Prayer

Queen of angels, pray for us!

October 23

Even some Catholics struggle to grasp My Mother's place in salvation history, in the Church, and in their own lives. But if they keep their eyes fixed on Me, they will understand her.

God's Word

". . . [A]t your right hand stands the queen in gold of Ophir" (Psalm 45:9).

Words of Wisdom

"Mary always held a special place in my heart, even in my years of rebellion when I didn't go to church. And now, as a religious, whenever I find myself in difficulty, rebelling in some way in my heart, I remember her words at the wedding feast of Cana, 'Do whatever He tells you.'" (Sr. Mary Ann Foggin, SGL, www.servantsofgodslove.catholicweb.com)

To Do

Pope Pius XII instituted the feast of the Queenship of Mary on August 22. Mary is Queen because Christ is King. "She indeed became mistress of all creation when she became mother of the Creator," says St. John Damascene. Pray the Litany of the Queenship of Mary.

To Journal

Women today are encouraged to act as divas and "queens." True queenship means servanthood, charity, mercy, and peace. *Noblesse oblige!* How can you live these virtues in imitation of Mary?

Prayer

Mystical rose, pray for us!

October 24

My Mother does not forget. My Mother keeps her promises.

 *God's Word*

". . . [M]y house shall be called a house of prayer for all peoples" (Isaiah 56:7).

Words of Wisdom

Muslims highly honor Mary. There are more words about her in the Koran than in the Gospels! This devotion to Mary came from Islam's Christian roots. Bishop Fulton Sheen believed that Muslims will eventually come to Jesus through Mary.

To do

From 1968 to 1971, Mary appeared above a church she had asked to be built in a 1918 apparition at El-Zeitoun, Egypt—the traditional site of the Flight into Egypt. Thousands of Christians and Muslims sang to her in Coptic, Arabic, and Greek. Jews and those of no faith saw her also. Research this rich series of apparitions of the "Mother of All Peoples." Mary is a prophet because prophets bring God's message; they don't necessarily foretell the future.

To journal

In these spectacular apparitions were lights, doves, colors, fragrances, and smoke. Mary was successively both sad and joyful. Mary and Jesus expressed the full range of human emotions. Do you? What emotions are hardest for you to express? Why?

Prayer

Queen of prophets, pray for us!

October 25

My Mother was not only My first disciple, but My first apostle. She brought Me in her womb to Elizabeth and John the Baptist. She presented Me to Joseph, the magi, and the shepherds.

God's Word

"All these with one accord devoted themselves to prayer, together with the women and Mary the mother of Jesus . . ." (Acts 1:14).

Words of Wisdom

"Never doubt the powerful prayers of the woman who knew Jesus better than anyone else on this earth; after all, she was His mother. Who can better lead us in prayer and teach us how to be true followers of Jesus?" (Sr. Maria Theotokos Adams, SSVM, www.ssvmusa.org/)

To Do

Bl. James Alberione and the Pauline Family honor Mary as Queen of Apostles. Read *Mary Leads Us to Jesus* by Alberione. Check out the Marian Library at the University of Dayton in Ohio, http://campus.udayton.edu/mary/library.html (the largest Marian library in the world). Check out film-depictions of Mary such as *Mary of Nazareth*, *Jesus* (a CBS mini-series), *The Nativity Story*, *Mary, Mother of Jesus*, and *The Passion of the Christ*.

To journal

How do you show Jesus to the world?

Prayer

Queen of apostles, pray for us!

October 26

I have made My Mother powerful against evil. Evil tries to oppose her, but also fears her.

God's Word

". . . [S]tanding by the cross of Jesus were his mother . . ." (John 19:25).

Words of Wisdom

Medieval art was very much into symbolism, including many symbols for Mary. Some were from the Bible, i.e., "the army set in array" (Song of Songs 6:3), and some were from nature (flowers such as columbine). If you learn more about Marian and other religious symbols, you'll be able to see Jesus and Mary all around you!

To Do

Mary was steadfast in the face of the worst evil the world has ever known: Deicide. Mary is powerful in spiritual warfare. Exorcists report that demons will curse everything and everyone, including Jesus, but are mysteriously prevented from ever cursing Mary. Research Spain's Our Lady of Pilar and Our Lady of Montserrat. Learn about Our Lady of Akita, Our Lady of China, and Our Lady of Africa.

To Journal

What are some symbols of Mary that you know of? Do you employ Mary in fighting your spiritual battles? How? When?

Prayer

Queen of martyrs, pray for us!

October 27

My Mother is very welcoming. And she loves visitors.

God's Word

"Woman, behold, your son!" (John 19:26)

Words of Wisdom

Mary must have been a very loving presence for Jesus' friends, especially after the Resurrection. The infancy narratives in the Gospels resulted from chats with Mary. We, too, can visit her whenever we want through the Rosary. It is a perfect prayer for sharing confidences. (Sr. Mary Lea Hill, FSP, www.daughtersofstpaul.org)

To Do

What is the Madonna of your ancestry? In the United States we honor Mary in her Immaculate Conception as our patroness. If you have a chance, visit the Basilica of the National Shrine of the Immaculate Conception in Washington, D.C. It's our national basilica. Is there a Marian shrine near you that you can visit? What is your parish's special devotion to Mary? Read the Vatican's document on the importance of shrines called *The Shrine: Memory, Presence and Prophecy* on www.vatican.va. Research Canada's Madonna, Our Lady of the Cape (Cap-de-la-Madeleine).

To Journal

What kind of Madonna does your city need (Our Lady of _____)? Your family? Your workplace? You? We can never have too many Madonnas!

Prayer

Queen of confessors, pray for us!

October 28

Although you may want to defend My Mother when she is dishonored, remember that people can be ignorant. Some may not even know what honor is, especially if they have never been treated with honor. My Mother is more interested in loving and honoring others than in defending herself.

God's word

"Mary said to the angel, 'How shall this be, since I have no husband?'" (Luke 1:34).

Words of wisdom

Respect is an honor to be aspired to, but it can easily slip into pride. Tribes and gangs demand respect, take offense, and retaliate at the least provocation. Respect is a virtue that should flow from a basic recognition of the human dignity of everyone.

To do

Check out Edgar Allen Poe's Marian poem entitled "Hymn," and the famous poem-prayer "Lovely Lady Dressed in Blue." Research other Marian poetry. Research Our Lady of Lujan.

To journal

If someone doesn't honor Mary, God, or the things of God, they are more to be pitied than punished. Are you overly sensitive to real or perceived offenses?

Prayer

Queen of virgins, pray for us!

October 29

When you say "Mary," she will respond with My name, "Jesus."

God's Word

"His mother said to the servants, 'Do whatever he tells you'" (John 2:5).

Words of Wisdom

Every honor to Mary is an honor for her Son. Make sure you have a Catholic liturgical calendar so you can celebrate Marian feast-days. Saturdays are dedicated to Mary, so you can celebrate her every Saturday also! Almost every day is a Marian feastday somewhere in the world. Learn about these many Marian feastdays (see "Calendar of Our Lady" in *The Essential Mary Handbook*). If Our Lady is Mother of God and Queen of the Universe, then she is "Our Lady of Everything and Everywhere"!

To do

Research Mary's house in Ephesus (modern-day Turkey), where it's believed she lived with St. John. Many Muslims go there to pray. To learn more, read *Mary's House* by Donald Carroll and watch *Mary's House—All Are Invited*.

To journal

What is your favorite way of addressing and speaking of Mary? Blessed Mother? Virgin Mary? Mother Mary? Our Lady? Why?

Prayer

Queen of all saints, pray for us!

October 30

My Mother's protection is mainly spiritual, but implore her for all your needs.

God's Word

"And his mercy is on those who fear him . . ." (Luke 1:50).

Words of Wisdom

See if your spirit is comforted and soaring at the same time when you invoke Mary's intercession! Memorize some of these standard Marian prayers of the Church: Angelus/Regina Caeli, Memorare, Hail Holy Queen, Hail Mary, Sub Tuum Praesidium, and Magnificat. Pray the lengthy Orthodox Marian prayer: "Akathist to the Theotokos" (literally "standing in prayer to the Mother of God").

To Do

Carry a rosary with you, or wear a rosary ring or bracelet. (It's easier to pray with a rosary ring or bracelet while walking, driving, or on a treadmill!) During the time of persecution in Ireland, the people hid one-decade rosaries in their pockets.

Research the Madonnas of ocean-travel, invoked by fishermen and sailors: Star of the Sea, Our Lady of Good Voyage, Our Lady of Caridad, Our Lady of Divine Providence, Our Lady of the Way. Learn the beautiful hymn in Latin or English: "Ave Maris Stella."

To Journal

When have you felt Mary's spiritual or physical protection?

Prayer

Mother most merciful, pray for us!

October 31

My peace will win in the end. Which side do you want to be on: the peaceful or the violent? Learn peace from My mother's heart.

God's word

". . . [H]is name will be called . . . 'Prince of Peace.' Of the increase of his government and of peace there will be no end . . ." (Isaiah 9:6–7). "The LORD . . . hates him that loves violence" (Psalm 11:5).

Words of wisdom

As the keepers and nurturers of life, women have a special part to play in keeping and promoting peace in the world. Is it really in woman's nature to be engaged in combat in war? Read Pope John Paul's message for World Day of Peace 1995: "Women: Teachers of Peace."

To do

Pray the Rosary for peace. The Bible begins and ends with Mary in a situation of conflict (cf. Genesis 3:15 and Revelation 12:13). She is no stranger to violence (think of the danger in her day of being pregnant outside wedlock, the murder of the Holy Innocents, the Flight into Egypt, the Crucifixion, the persecution of the early Church). Learn about Our Lady of Medjugorje, Our Lady of Peace.

To journal

Do you spread peace wherever you go? How?

Prayer

Queen of peace, pray for us!

November 1

I call everyone to celibacy if they're not called to marriage. Those who are called to marriage are called to celibacy until they're married.

God's Word

"Blessed are the pure in heart, for they shall see God" (Matthew 5:8).

Words of Wisdom

Celibacy is continence, abstaining from sexual intercourse. *Chastity* is purity, or expressing love and one's sexuality according to one's state of life. Everyone is called to chastity, including the married. Celibacy *is* an expression of love and sexuality because we are sexual beings simply by being male or female!

To Do

There are many natural and supernatural helps to living celibacy: exercise, hobbies, devotion to Our Lady, friendships, work, Eucharistic Adoration, and volunteering. Read *The Courage to be Chaste* by Fr. Benedict Groeschel, CFR—one of the best books on the art of celibate living with pizzazz!

To Journal

Do you feel you're called to permanent celibacy or to marriage? If permanent celibacy, do you feel you're called to religious life or single life? How can religious live their sexuality appropriately? How can a single person?

Prayer

Dear Jesus, living chastely is one of life's biggest challenges. Help!

November 2

If you ever forget that following Me is arduous, your call to chastity will remind you.

God's word

"If any man would come after me, let him deny himself . . ." (Luke 9:23). "Do not follow your base desires, but restrain your appetites" (Sirach 18:30). "Lust indulged starves the soul . . ." (Proverbs 13:19 NAB).

Words of wisdom

Your Baptism has marked you for heroism. The Christian life is like a video game with only one level: expert. We don't get to choose mediocre. Unfair? Not when you've been equipped to succeed. The good news is that Jesus will always assist us, and when we fall, forgive us, and get us started on our way again.

To do

Did you know that movie superheroes are quite often celibate? Why do you think this is so? Watch *Van Helsing*. At the end, what does he sacrifice himself for?

To journal

Who are your favorite real-life heroes or fantasy superheroes? Why? What are their strengths and weaknesses? What great celibates have you known personally or admired from a distance?

Prayer

Dear Jesus, I don't think of myself as a hero, or even called to be one. But I guess my struggles with chastity could put me in that category!

November 3

I created you as a sexual being. Don't run from this fact, embrace it.

God's Word

"There is no fear in love, but perfect love casts out fear" (1 John 4:18). "For fear is nothing but surrender of the helps that come from reason . . ." (Wisdom 17:12).

Words of Wisdom

When God made creation, He called it "good." When God made human beings, He called us "very good"! Sexuality is meant to be strong because it is an expression of God's strong love for us. Our bodies, our sexuality are in the image of God and we are co-creators with Him of new human life. Reflect often on the goodness of your sexuality!

To Do

Don't be afraid of your sexuality. Although it's a very powerful force, you can learn to channel it properly with God's help.

To Journal

What are your fears with regard to your sexuality? How can you live the "redemption of the body" (not the repression or indulgence of the body)?

Prayer

Dear Jesus, please heal any fear I have of my sexuality.

November 4

Do you rejoice in My gift of sexuality? I rejoice in your rejoicing.

"Behold, you are beautiful, my love, behold, you are beautiful!" (Song of Songs 4:1)

Words of wisdom

It's good not to be afraid of our sexuality, but we must also maintain a healthy respect for its depth and power.

To do

Write out your "sexual history"—that is, your general attitude and experiences of your own sexuality so far. Have you centered your sexuality in God? Is there a need for Confession or change here?

To journal

Different people experience different intensities of their "sex drive." Does yours tend to be high or low? How does this affect your living the virtue of chastity? How are you helping yourself to live chastity?

Prayer

Dear Jesus, help me live my sexuality with wisdom, maturity, and holiness.

November 5

Celibacy is not a "virtue," but can be an orientation of your entire life.

God's word

". . . [T]here are eunuchs who have made themselves eunuchs for the sake of the kingdom of heaven" (Matthew 19:12).

Words of wisdom

If you are celibate because you believe in the teachings of Jesus, then you are "celibate for the kingdom of God" similar to a consecrated religious. The call is essentially the same, even if you eventually intend to get married. Read the text of John Paul II's *Man and Woman He Created Them: A Theology of the Body* on "Continence for the Kingdom of Heaven."

To do

Do you know someone in the seminary? On his way to priesthood, he will become a transitional deacon (as opposed to a permanent deacon). If you are planning on getting married, think of yourself as a "transitional celibate"!

To journal

What do you think are the differences "transitional celibates" experience in practicing celibacy from "permanent celibates"? What do you think are the differences male celibates experience in practicing celibacy from female celibates?

Prayer

Dear Jesus, with regard to my living of celibacy temporarily or permanently, please be my peace.

November 6

If you love someone, but aren't married to them, why can't you express your love by having sex with them? Precisely because you say you love them.

God's word

"So they are no longer two but one flesh. What therefore God has joined together, let not man put asunder" (Matthew 19:6).

Words of wisdom

Animals have sex. Human beings commit publicly and permanently to each other in love. Some think we should always call sex "the marital embrace" so it can never be separated from marriage. Science says that sex bonds us physically to our sexual partner. Sex is marriage and marriage is sex.

To do

Learn more about Jesus's and the Church's teaching on sexuality, especially if you don't understand the principles involved.

To journal

Copy this thought from Epictetus, the first-century pagan philosopher: Sex is not something to be played with as if a game; it engages our deepest emotions and has very real consequences. By turning a deaf ear to this advice we debase ourselves and cheapen our relationships.

Prayer

Dear Jesus, okay, I get it: "Love isn't a fantasy in silk and lace, love is a commitment, face to face" (Larry Norman).

November 7

You are My witness. Martyrdom is the greatest witness. Celibacy and chastity are a type of daily martyrdom.

God's word

"Have no anxiety about anything" (Philippians 4:6).

Words of wisdom

You are not alone in your struggle to live chastely. It is a noble fight. When it comes to sexual temptations, do not be anxious, it only exacerbates the temptation. Don't take yourself too seriously. That *definitely* exacerbates the temptation!

To do

Learn all you can about the vocation to the single life. If you think you're going to be single for a while, join a singles group.

To journal

Often we expect our life's pathway to be strewn with roses. However, we forget that even roses are born of sun *and* rain. Country songs can be very helpful when dealing with chastity issues. What are some lines from country songs (or love songs) that apply?

Prayer

Dear Jesus, by Your constant love, free me from all anxiety as I joyfully await Your return in glory.

November 8

There has always been opposition to celibacy and chastity. Welcome to the history of the world.

God's Word

"Submit yourselves therefore to God. Resist the devil and he will flee from you" (James 4:7).

Words of Wisdom

Some define a celibate person as unhealthy, unbalanced, and not well-adjusted, but wouldn't that assessment apply to someone *incapable* of celibacy, someone incapable of self-control? Before Christ and Mary, only fertility had meaning for most of the world. Now celibacy as a life-commitment has great meaning!

To Do

In *The Courage to be Chaste*, Fr. Groeschel offers a four-step procedure for dealing with sexual temptation: 1) tell yourself "this is a temptation"; 2) try to understand where the temptation is coming from *now* (analysis kills lust!); 3) pray; 4) stop whatever you're doing and do something else, even change environments.

To Journal

Celibacy and chastity are areas of our lives where we will probably have failures as well as victories. We must neither excuse ourselves nor despair. What have my failures and victories in celibacy and chastity taught me?

Prayer

Dear Jesus, I'm leaning on You for this one. Teach me humility when I fail and courage to continue the fight.

November 9

I did not create you as an angel. You cannot live without your sexuality—that complex, intimate, intricate part of who you are.

God's Word

"The heart is deceitful above all things . . . who can understand it?" (Jeremiah 17:9)

Words of Wisdom

Instead of always thinking of chastity in terms of sin, it is helpful to think in terms of goals. When you fail, tell Jesus "I've hurt myself," because, ultimately, sin is a form of self-hatred.

To do

Remember that living our sexuality is like climbing a mountain. We just keep putting one foot in front of the other, and eventually we'll get to the top. It's important to know that temptations, thoughts, dreams, feelings, even occasions of unintended arousal, are not sinful. It's what we do with them.

To journal

A surfer-priest in California developed the "five second look." When he sees a beautiful woman on the beach, he looks for five seconds (without lusting), appreciates her God-given beauty, then looks away and gets on with surfing! What are some ways you help yourself live chastely?

Prayer

Dear Jesus, I don't want to be an angel. I want to be a woman. Your woman.

November 10

Do people tell you celibacy and chastity are unhealthy, abnormal, and impossible? Will you listen to them or to Me?

God's Word

"What is impossible with men is possible with God" (Luke 18:27).

Words of wisdom

No one ever died from celibacy. It is not necessary to act out every potentiality of our person to be fully alive. What is imperative is that we make a gift of ourselves in love. The freedom of celibacy provides excellent opportunities to do just that!

To do

We love either as a man loves or as a woman loves. It's different! Explore what it means that celibates make a gift of themselves either as a man or a woman.

To journal

Opponents to celibacy are correct in saying it's impossible . . . *without God*. (And if someone thinks they're living celibacy by their own steam, they are either deluded or what they're living isn't true celibacy but some kind of frigidity.) What are other things you know you could never do without God's help?

Prayer

Dear Jesus, St. Irenaeus says that "the glory of God is the human person fully alive." Teach me to be fully alive by being the fully loving woman I am.

November 11

I created the naked human body beautiful, but the fallen world can't appreciate it properly.

God's word

"And the man and his wife were both naked, and were not ashamed" (Genesis 2:25).

Words of wisdom

Since we live in a fallen world, we must still clothe our bodies from the lusts of others (cf. Romans 8:23). The difference between love and lust is that love sees the whole person, desires that person's good, and would never hurt them, while lust sees a thing to use for one's own sinful gratification.

To do

There is a world of difference between true art and pornography. Pornography presents (mostly) women as unrealistic objects of lust, creates a sinful atmosphere for all involved in its production and use, de-personalizes and dehumanizes, replaces relationships with fantasies, stimulates addictions, and destroys innocence and intimacy. Read the section in John Paul's *Man and Women He Created Them: A Theology of the Body* on "The Ethos of the Body in Art and Media."

To journal

List other reasons why pornography is so destructive.

Prayer

Dear Jesus, give me a great respect for my body and the bodies of others. May I always see You reflected in the human body.

November 12

Are you single? Misunderstood? Maligned? Don't worry. I was too.

God's Word

"... [D]o not throw your pearls before swine ..." (Matthew 7:6).

Words of Wisdom

"Sometimes chastity can be lonely because we stand in the minority. Chastity, however, is one of the greatest gifts; it is both rewarding and leaves us with great peace of soul. Don't throw this precious pearl before the swine, because cleaning up their mess is stinky and sometimes impossible!" (Sr. Colleen Clair, FMA, www.salesiansisterseast.org)

To Do

Develop a sense of humor about singleness. Are you mocked for your singleness, celibacy, or chastity? (People can be nosy, rude, and clueless in this regard.) Create some stock phrases like: "Any time I want, I can become like you, but you can't become like me!" If people harass you about not having sex, simply remind them that you're a Christian (they probably are too) and let that sink in.

To Journal

Which feels more natural for you: celibacy or married life?

Prayer

Dear Jesus, so many people resolve their sexual tension by "going with the flow." But even a dead salmon can go with the flow. Help me make the effort and give me the grace to swim upstream.

November 13

Some were given the grace to recognize celibacy as a fruitful way of life even before My Incarnation.

God's Word

". . . God shows no partiality, but in every nation any one who fears him and does what is right is acceptable to him" (Acts 10:34–35). "For I am not ashamed of the gospel . . ." (Romans 1:16).

Words of Wisdom

Sometimes those who reject the call to celibacy or have given up trying to live it go on a rampage against those who are still trying. If people attack your faith in regard to celibacy, you can remind them that celibacy is much bigger and older than Christianity.

To Do

Watch *Kundun,* about the life of the Dalai Lama, *Dead Man Walking*, about Sr. Helen Prejean, CSJ, *The Painted Veil*, and *Keeping the Faith*. How is religious celibacy recognized as a gift in these films? How does it bear fruit?

To Journal

Think of certain artists, doctors, explorers, athletes, and others who practice celibacy for non-religious reasons. How is even non-religious celibacy a fruitful gift?

Prayer

Dear Jesus, celibacy—because it's a good thing—is recognized by the intellectually honest and pure of heart. Let me never be ashamed of it.

November 14

It was My love for you that drove Me to the cross.

God's Word

". . . [A]s the bridegroom rejoices over the bride, so shall your God rejoice over you" (Isaiah 62:5). "Jesus . . . for the joy that was set before him endured the cross . . ." (Hebrews 12:2).

Words of Wisdom

John Paul II tells us we need to be fully aware of our options in order to make a mature choice of either married or celibate life. He says that although celibacy for the kingdom is oriented to the next life, it still has significance for this life in its "style, value, and evangelical authenticity" (*Man and Woman He Created Them*, 81:4).

To do

If we undervalue marriage or cease to look to marriage as the primordial human relationship, we will lose sight of God's passionate, concrete love for us. Research the Shakers—an eighteenth-century religious movement that was confused about celibacy (and basically died out!). Read *The Jeweler's Shop* by Pope John Paul II about marriage. Look up Eastern icons of "Christ the Bridegroom." Why do they depict Jesus's Passion?

To journal

How do you live your celibacy with style?

Prayer

Dear Jesus, direct all my desires to You.

November 15

I chose celibacy for Myself.

God's Word

"You are the fairest of the sons of men . . ." (Psalm 45:2).

Words of Wisdom

John Paul II says that even though men are directed toward women and women are directed toward men, we are able to discover in our solitude "a fuller form of inter-subjective communion with others." When we "choose continence for the kingdom of heaven," we can realize ourselves differently, by becoming "a sincere gift for others" (cf. *Man and Woman He Created Them*, 77:2).

To do

Jesus's choice of celibacy was a break with the tradition of the Old Testament. Celibacy's real value is when it is "for the kingdom of God," not because it is abstention from sex. Continence as a response to the Divine Bridegroom is itself an act of spousal love. Consider how you are living your life "for the sake of the kingdom."

To journal

In a sense, celibates and religious are free to have a "love for strangers," for those who have no family or friends to love them. When have you reached out to strangers? When have they reached out to you?

Prayer

Dear Jesus, You desire me. Keep my desire for You always burning.

November 16

The call to celibacy is a unique call to participate in the establishment of My kingdom on earth.

God's Word

". . . [T]he unmarried woman or girl is anxious about the affairs of the Lord, how to be holy in body and spirit . . ." (1 Corinthians 7:34).

Words of Wisdom

The Apostle Paul wrote the above words to the sexually-corrupt city of Corinth. He was well aware that our bodies are "temple[s] of the Holy Spirit," but also fragile "earthen vessels." Paul was so excited about the coming kingdom that he urged *all* to consider celibacy for that kingdom! "The world in its present form is passing away" (cf. 1 Corinthians 6:19, 2 Corinthians 4:7, 1 Corinthians 7:31).

To do

"For Christ did not please himself . . ." (Romans 15:3). ". . . I always do what is pleasing to him [the Father]" (John 8:29). Name how it is that you seek to please the Lord.

To journal

We are all anxious about whatever is in our hearts. What's in your heart?

Prayer

Dear Jesus, may the thoughts of my mind be pleasing to You, and the words of my mouth find favor before You.

November 17

In their bodies men show forth My transcendence best; women show forth My immanence best.

God's Word

"This is my beloved and this is my friend, O daughters of Jerusalem" (Song of Songs 5:16).

Words of Wisdom

One of the most important things we can do in life is understand who we are as women, our feminine identity in Christ. To talk about woman's "role" can imply something imposed or put on that is not natural to us. We simply want to be who we are as the women God created us to be.

To Do

Even if one is single or enters religious life, one is still fully a woman! What are the best things about being a woman? Do you struggle with your femininity? Pray for the healing of your understanding of your femininity. Do you struggle with same-sex attraction? Check out www.couragerc.net.

To Journal

What are some ways men and women image God differently? What are some ways men and women experience God differently? What are some ways men and women love differently?

Prayer

Dear Jesus, I thank You for making me a woman. Help me continue to discover and live my femininity.

November 18

There is no such thing as "the feminine divine" or "the masculine divine." Sexuality is My gift to human beings.

God's Word

"For as the heavens are higher than the earth, so are my ways higher than your ways and my thoughts than your thoughts" (Isaiah 55:9).

Words of Wisdom

To say that God must possess something in order to give it is to limit God. Sex applies to humans, not God. Jesus has two natures: divine and human. He is masculine in His human nature only.

To do

Mary is not a stand-in or replacement for "the goddess." Mary models for the whole human race how to be a child of the Father, yield to the Holy Spirit, and be the perfect disciple and apostle of Jesus. Take the time to clear up wrong-headed ideas about masculinity and femininity, both earthly and heavenly!

To journal

What false images and notions of Mary make it hard to relate to her? Does it have something to do with your own idea of motherhood or experience of femininity?

Prayer

Dear Jesus, I praise You that one day we will be fully redeemed, glorified, and "Christified" as Mary is now in heaven!

November 19

Even if you don't feel Me calling you to religious life, learn about it. You can be a great support to friends or your own children someday.

God's word

"There were also many women there . . . who had followed Jesus from Galilee, ministering to him . . ." (Matthew 27:55).

Words of wisdom

God has loved us from before the creation of the universe, from before *our* creation. He loves us with an everlasting love. Religious life might seem like the ultimate delayed gratification, but really, God's the One who has been waiting for us for such a long time.

To do

You already know what single life is. You know what family life is. But do you really know what religious life is? Go on a vocation "Come and See" day, or talk with some sisters you know. Read *When God Asks for an Undivided Heart* by Fr. Andrew Apostoli, CFR or *And You Are Christ's* by Fr. Thomas Dubay. Check out www.cmswr.org, www.religiouslife.org.

To journal

What are my questions about religious life? What are things I don't understand or find most mysterious about religious life?

Prayer

Dear Jesus, if I'm not called to religious life, let me encourage those who are.

November 20

Why chastity, poverty, and obedience? Because they correspond to sex, money, and power.

God's word

". . . [T]he lust of the flesh and the lust of the eyes and the pride of life, is not of the Father but is of the world" (1 John 2:16).

Words of wisdom

Religious live the "evangelical counsels" which are suggestions rather than commandments. Religious make vows of chastity, poverty, and obedience in order to free themselves from the threefold concupiscence of life—and help sex, money, and power serve God and neighbor.

To do

Everyone lives the evangelical counsels in some way. Everyone has to live some form of chastity. How many people have all the money they want (poverty)? (And the rich are called to share with the poor.) We all obey laws and authorities (obedience). Examine *your* living of the evangelical counsels.

To journal

In the past, the order of the vows were: poverty, chastity, and obedience. But now it's: chastity, poverty, and obedience. Why do you think this was changed? Write down ways a religious can give and receive love.

Prayer

Dear Jesus, please uphold all religious in the life to which they were called and which they chose to follow.

November 21

Love makes all things sweeter and easier.

"He who is able to receive this, let him receive it" (Matthew 19:12).

Words of wisdom

John Paul II doesn't hide the serious commitment that vowed celibate life is. He uses words like travail, self-sacrifice, renunciation, responsibility, effort, cross, self-denial, and momentousness. (And he admits these exist in marriage, too!) But then he notes that "what shines and gleams is love: love as the readiness to make the exclusive gift of self for the kingdom of heaven."

To do

"It is a characteristic feature of the human heart to accept even difficult demands in the name of love, for an ideal, and above all in the name of love for a person (love is, in fact, oriented by its very nature toward the person)" (*Man and Woman He Created Them*, 79:9). Listen to 10cc's song "The Things We Do for Love." Listen to U2's "Pride (In the Name of Love)."

To journal

"Love does such things." What are you willing to do for love?

Prayer

Dear Jesus, may I live more and more out of love. May love become my motivation in all things.

November 22

I gave you three different metaphors for the kingdom of heaven. But no one can be all three at the same time.

God's Word

"The kingdom of heaven is like leaven" (Matthew 13:33). "A city set on a hill cannot be hid. . . . A lamp . . . gives light to all in the house" (Matthew 5:14–15).

Words of Wisdom

Laity are most like the leaven in the dough. *Religious* are most like the lamp. The *bishops and priests* are most like the city on the hill.

To do

At our Baptism, we are anointed *priests, prophets, and kings* like Jesus. Laity best reflect the *priesthood* of Jesus by offering the daily world back to God. Religious reflect the *prophetic* mission of Jesus by living the evangelical counsels and the spirit of the early Church. The bishops and priests (hierarchy) best reflect the *kingship* of Jesus by governing and sanctifying. Renew your baptismal promises today.

To journal

You were anointed at Baptism. You are royalty. What will you do with your anointing?

Prayer

Dear Jesus, if I ever wonder if I'm authorized to represent You, to speak or act in Your name, I'll just remind myself that I have been *anointed*!

November 23

Do you truly value all the vocations in My Church?

God's Word

". . . [E]ach has his own special gift from God . . ." (1 Corinthians 7:7).

Words of Wisdom

Why is it that people will ask a religious sister, "Aw, didn't you want to get married?" but never ask a married woman, "Aw, didn't you want to be a sister?" It's said that St. Ambrose was such an effective preacher of virginity as a way of life that parents would lock up their daughters when he came to town to preach!

To Do

Celibacy is not primarily negative, it's positive. It means seeking God and God alone. God did not give us sexual desires in order to frustrate us. Rather, he will transform them and fulfill them completely, body and soul, in heaven in a new and deeper way. Enumerate for yourself what you personally find positive about celibacy.

To Journal

What is there about the state of life you're *not* called to that you will miss?

Prayer

Dear Jesus, help me to appreciate the married, single, and religious life as gifts from You.

November 24

The structure I gave My Church is complementary, like the human body.

God's Word

". . . [A]ll the members of the body, though many, are one body, so it is with Christ" (1 Corinthians 12:12). ". . . [T]here are many parts, yet one body" (1 Corinthians 12:20).

Words of Wisdom

Think of your vocation as part gift, part call, and part choice.

To do

The internal life of the Church should be a mutual admiration society! We are inextricably linked together: priests, religious, laity. A married laywoman said, "I believe that the sisters are a spiritual cover for us married people. When the sisters lose their way, married people do, too." Read *Sisters in Crisis* by Ann Carey to understand what happened in religious life in the United States after Vatican II.

To journal

G. K. Chesterton once said, "When monasteries return, marriages will return." What did he mean by this?

Prayer

Dear Jesus, let us, Your Mystical Body, always be of help and support to one another, especially through our prayer.

November 25

Are you unsure if your calling is married life or celibate life? Maybe that's because they're so similar.

God's word
". . . [L]et every one lead the life which the Lord has assigned to him, and in which God has called him" (1 Corinthians 7:17).

Words of wisdom
If you've chosen the single life yet are consistently unhappy because of it, you may want to reconsider. Whatever your calling, you are called to make a gift of yourself to God and others.

To do
Be careful of self-pity in your living of celibacy. Are you generous? Cultivating friendships? Getting involved in the community? Sharing your time, treasure, and talent? If we sow sparingly, we will reap sparingly (cf. 2 Corinthians 9:6). Do temptations come when you're feeling sorry for yourself or entitled?

To journal
Loneliness is experienced in every vocation. We cannot expect anyone else to be God for us and fulfill all our needs and longings. Married couples can be lonely even when they're together. How do you deal with loneliness?

Prayer
Dear Jesus, help me remember "there is more joy in giving than in receiving." Help me to be as concerned about fulfilling others' needs as fulfilling my own.

November 26

My celibacy and preaching of celibacy for the sake of the kingdom did not change the value of marriage.

God's word

"... [A]s Christ loved the church and gave himself up for her ... husbands should love their wives as their own bodies" (Ephesians 5:25, 28).

Words of wisdom

Jesus made it clear that the call to religious celibacy was not ordinary or universal. It was an exception for those who "understand," for those called.

To do

John Paul II says that "the perfection of Christian life is measured by the measure of love" (*Man and Woman He Created Them*, 78:3). He says that it's possible for married people to live love more perfectly than a vowed religious. Whoever loves more "wins"! Choose a married couple and a religious celibate you know as your models of love.

To journal

Pope John Paul II says that the vocations to marriage and continence "complete each other and in some sense interpenetrate." They are both based on the "faithfulness and gift of the one and only Bridegroom . . . to the one and only Bride" (*Man and Woman He Created Them*, 78:4). What does this mean to you?

Prayer

Dear Jesus, I want more of Your love, more of Your power, more of You in my life.

November 27

Marriage and celibacy will both be taken to a deeper level in heaven.

God's Word

"For when they rise from the dead, they neither marry nor are given in marriage" (Mark 12:25).

Words of Wisdom

Marriage is communion with God and each other (the couple). *Celibacy* is communion with God and each other (the whole human family). *Heaven* is communion with God and each other (the communion of saints).

To do

Married couples love God in an *inclusive* way: God *and* family. They love their family in an *exclusive* way (as their first duty before everybody else). Celibates love God in an *exclusive* way: God *alone*. They love the human family in an *inclusive* way (everybody is their first duty!). Think about these realities as you consider your call to love.

To journal

Single people have a serious duty to reach out! But we can only reach out in love when we feel loved ourselves and are firmly rooted in the source of all love. Prayer is essential to this. What are some ways to give and receive love as a single person?

Prayer

Dear Jesus, teach me that giving and receiving can be simultaneous.

November 28

Raw might and brute force are not true power. True power is found in mutual service, humility, and love.

God's Word

"Joseph . . . do not fear to take Mary your wife, for that which is conceived in her is of the Holy Spirit" (Matthew 1:20).

Words of wisdom

"The marriage of Mary with Joseph . . . conceals . . . the mystery of the perfect communion of persons . . . in the conjugal covenant and at the same time the mystery of this singular 'continence for the kingdom of heaven'" (*Man and Woman He Created Them*, 75:3). Let the Holy Family be a model for whatever form of community you live.

To do

Read *Guardian of the Redeemer*, Pope John Paul II's letter on St. Joseph. If you ever get within 5,000 miles of beautiful St. Joseph's Oratory in Montreal, go. Watch *Joseph of Nazareth*.

To journal

St. Joseph is patron of the universal Church, families, marriages, the dying, the poor, work and workers, carpenters, and a provider of material needs. The Church has long cried: "Ite ad Joseph! (Go to Joseph!)" How is Joseph the model for all men?

Prayer

Dear Jesus, bless all families. May they not be places of struggle for power, but of love.

November 29

Both the married and the celibate have to give up something beautiful. But both have spousal love.

God's Word

"And the unmarried woman . . . is anxious about the affairs of the Lord . . . but the married woman is anxious about worldly affairs, how to please her husband" (1 Corinthians 7:34).

Words of Wisdom

Pope John Paul II says marriage illumines celibacy and vice versa. Marriage is understood in relation to "the beginning" (creation), and celibacy for the kingdom is understood in relation to "the end" (fullness of redemption).

To do

Write down your personal pros and cons for each vocation. Pope John Paul II makes it clear that it is not as though marriage is carnal and celibacy is spiritual. They are both carnal *and* spiritual because, no matter our vocation, we participate in it body and soul. (If we look down on what is carnal, it shows that we do not see the body as good!)

To journal

Marriage and celibacy both provide a full answer to the question about the meaning of "being a body," that is, the meaning of masculinity and femininity. What are your questions about "being a body"? (*Man and Woman He Created Them*, 85:9)

Prayer

Dear Jesus, help me be faithful to "my own gift."

November 30

My redemption transforms every aspect of your life, including your sexuality.

God's Word

"For I do not do the good I want, but the evil I do not want. . . . Who will deliver me from this body of death? Thanks be to God through Jesus Christ our Lord!" (Romans 7:19, 24–25) "And we . . . are being changed into his likeness from one degree of glory to another" (2 Corinthians 3:18).

Words of Wisdom

Pope John Paul II says that we don't have to wait until heaven to be victorious in Jesus. We can be victorious here and now by drawing strength from the mystery of the "redemption of the body." Jesus invites us to overcome sinfulness, even the "exclusively inner movements of the human heart" (cf. Matthew 5:27–28; *Man and Woman He Created Them*, 86:6).

To Do

We live "everyday hope" especially in our commitments as married, single, or religious. How can you live hope more fully? How do you express hope in the nitty-gritty details of your day? Read Pope Benedict's encyclical, *Saved in Hope*.

To Journal

What victory over sin, what "everyday hope" do you need? Which ones do you celebrate?

Prayer

Dear Jesus, conquer all of me. I surrender.

December 1

Pretend you are already in eternity with Me. Look backwards at your life. How short it was!

God's Word

". . . [I]f I deliver my body to be burned, but have not love, I gain nothing" (1 Corinthians 13:3). ". . . [W]hen the perfect comes, the imperfect will pass away" (1 Corinthians 13:10).

Words of wisdom

The Church has traditionally spoken of "the four last things," that is: death, judgment, heaven, and hell. Purgatory won't last, and although death and judgment are one-time events, their outcomes are permanent. Heaven and hell can be thought of as both states and places, but not in a way we have ever experienced.

To do

Check out this very helpful webpage: http://www.cuf.org/FaithFacts/details_view.asp?ffID=68

Read the *Catechism of the Catholic Church* (nos. 981–1060). Read *The Last Things* by Regis Martin.

To journal

St. Therese was asked what she thought of in her quiet moments, and she said, "Eternity." How often do you think about "the four last things"? Do you think about them with fear or with trust in God?

Prayer

Lord, open your heaven to all who have died. Let them live in perpetual joy and peace with You.

December 2

What will everyone be judged on at the end of life? Love.

God's word

"For God will bring every deed into judgment, with every secret thing, whether good or evil" (Ecclesiastes 12:14).

Words of wisdom

There are two judgments. The "particular judgment" of each soul immediately after death when the *soul* goes to purgatory, heaven, or hell to await reunion with the body. The "general/final/last judgment" at the end of the world is when everyone will receive again their *bodies* which will share in the good or evil they have done, and then go to heaven or hell.

To do

We need to exercise the virtue of hope when we think of judgment. The lyrics from Michael Card's song "Jubilee" say, "To be so completely guilty, given over to despair, to look into your Judge's face and see a Savior there." Look up his song, "There's a Wideness in God's Mercy."

To journal

The Scriptures often speak of the judgment in terms of court proceedings. Who is the advocate? Who is the accuser? Journal about how you feel about the judgment.

Prayer

"The trumpet casts a wondrous sound, through the tombs of all around, making them the throne surround" (*Dies Irae*).

December 3

If you ask Me to remember your sins which I have forgiven, I will say, "I forgot."

God's word

"And the dead were judged by what was written in the books" (Revelation 20:12).

Words of wisdom

God is merciful and just. God cannot give heaven to those who are incapable of appreciating or enjoying heaven which is God Himself.

To do

At the judgment we will get exactly what we want, therefore, it's important to desire the right things, above all, God! Read *The Great Divorce* by C. S. Lewis. God doesn't *send* anyone to heaven or hell. We go where we want to go. We go where we belong.

To journal

If we are examining our conscience well now, we won't have any surprises then. Write down these questions regarding sin: Was it serious? Did I know it was serious? Did I give full consent? Am I sorry? Did I go to Confession? Did I resolve not to do it again? Did I make restitution?

Prayer

"O good Jesus, have mercy on us: because You created us, You have redeemed us with Your Precious Blood" ("*O Bone Jesu*").

December 4

Your spiritual work continues in the next life. Purgatory is the final preparation for the beatific vision, My love without end.

God's Word

". . . [E]ach man's work will become manifest; for the Day will disclose it . . . the fire will test what sort of work each one has done" (1 Corinthians 3:13).

Words of Wisdom

Pray for the holy souls in purgatory frequently. They intercede for you as you do for them. They are no longer able to help themselves, but you can help them.

To do

Learn about that place or state where most of us will go immediately after death: purgatory. Pray for the holy souls in purgatory using Susan Tassone's prayerbooks.

To journal

We need to be ready to receive the ultimate gift: eternal life with God on high! Purgatory is worth it! Purgatory means you "made it"! Write about how it must feel to be separated from God after seeing him at death, knowing that you will see him again because you are *saved*.

Prayer

Lord, forgive the sins of all the departed and welcome them into your heavenly kingdom.

December 5

I created you for heaven, nothing less. Whatever meaning, purpose, truth, goodness, pleasure, and beauty you may find in this life, it's just a pale beginning of what awaits you.

God's Word

". . . God will wipe away every tear from their eyes" (Revelation 7:17).

Words of Wisdom

Think often about heaven, it puts everything in perspective. The more you think about heaven, the stronger your desire for it will become.

To Do

The greatest injustice done to God and human beings is to make heaven a dull and boring place of clouds, harps, and white gowns. No wonder few are interested in going there. Read *A Travel Guide to Heaven* by Anthony DeStefano, and you'll definitely want to go there.

To Journal

Who are the people and what are the things you love most? Describe the joy you feel from these people, things, and activities. Now multiply that to an infinite degree, one that just keeps growing and growing forever. That's heaven.

Prayer

"Abode of pure delights unmingled with sorrow. Where the affections always are satisfied and free from all fear. Where our God will wipe away every sorrow and every tear" (*"Paradiso"*).

December 6

The Evil One "created" hell for himself because he chose not to be with Me. He invites you to join him.

God's word

"And they shall go forth and look on the dead bodies of the men that have rebelled against me; for their worm shall not die, their fire shall not be quenched, and they shall be an abhorrence to all flesh" (Isaiah 66:24).

Words of wisdom

Could hell be devoid of humans? The Church has never pronounced that anyone is definitely in hell. Not even Judas.

To do

The greatest injustice is to make hell an exciting place—like a devil-themed Las Vegas club, where "all my friends are going anyway!" No wonder nobody fears going there. In reality Heaven is ecstasy. Hell is hatred (no friendship in hell!), pain, and regret.

To journal

What are your greatest fears, most horrible memories, pains, feelings? What are the most evil things that have happened in history? Now multiply that to an infinite degree that just keeps growing and growing forever. That's hell.

Prayer

"Give me a place among the sheep, separate from the goats, setting me at Your right hand" (*"Dies Irae"*).

December 7

I am the Way to the Father. I am all mercy. Trust in My mercy toward everyone.

God's Word

"Turn to me and be saved, all the ends of the earth!" (Isaiah 45:22)

Words of Wisdom

God wants all to be saved. His will is a saving will. He makes sure that everyone has ample opportunity, ways, and means to choose Him. There are three different kinds of Baptism: Baptism of water, desire, and blood. Baptism of desire refers to those who live according to their conscience and who would have chosen Jesus had they understood who he is. Baptism of blood refers to those who have not yet received Baptism of water and give their life for the faith.

To do

Find out the date of your Baptism. How can you commemorate it each year? Read more about Baptism in the *Catechism of the Catholic Church* (nos. 1257–1261).

To journal

Make a list of friends and famous people (living and dead) who might have the "Baptism of desire."

Prayer

"You who absolved Mary Magdalene, and heard the robber, have given me hope as well" (*"Dies Irae"*).

December 8

All are alive to Me. My gift of life, of being, is a forever gift. No one goes out of existence or ceases to exist.

God's Word

". . . [W]hether we live or whether we die, we are the Lord's" (Romans 14:8). "Precious in the sight of the LORD is the death of his faithful ones" (Psalm 116:15 NRSV).

Words of Wisdom

As soon as we begin to live, we begin to die. This may be temporarily true of our organic bodies (which will then be resurrected), but not of our immortal souls. Life is not about dying, it's about more life. Life is a vocation. We are *called* to eternal life.

To do

". . . [B]e the more zealous to confirm your call and election . . ." (2 Peter 1:10). ". . . I have set before you life and death . . . choose life . . ." (Deuteronomy 30:19). Choose life.

To journal

Elizabeth Kubler-Ross, in her book *On Death and Dying*, identified five stages of dying: denial, anger, bargaining, depression, and acceptance. People also go through these stages when facing change. Do they look familiar to you? When?

Prayer

Lord, may St. Michael, Your standard-bearer, lead the dead into the kingdom You promised to Abraham and his children forever.

December 9

Do you wish to see Me? Do you wish for special signs? I especially bless those who believe although they have seen nothing.

God's word

"Without having seen him you love him; though you do not now see him you believe in him and rejoice with unutterable and exalted joy" (1 Peter 1:8).

Words of wisdom

Some people report near-death experiences during accidents or operations. God gives each person what he knows they need. If you haven't had any extraordinary experiences, take it as a compliment. God just might think your faith is strong enough!

To do

People often say the most meaningful and revealing things as they die, summing up what is truly important in life. Find out how grandparents and relatives died. What were some of their last words? Do an online search for "famous last words." What do they reveal?

To journal

St. Paul reports being taken up to the "third heaven." Do you know anyone who has had a near-death experience? What glimpses of heaven do you believe you've been given without a near-death experience?

Prayer

Dear Jesus, let Your just ones live forever in our memory as examples of Your grace and mercy.

December 10

Imagination is one of My most precious gifts. Using your imagination will help you when you read the Bible.

God's Word

". . . [T]oday you will be with me in Paradise" (Luke 23:43).

Words of Wisdom

In a sense, Dante and Milton were like the sci-fi writers of their day, exploring the ramifications of Scripture and "all that is seen and unseen." Dante takes us on a journey through hell, purgatory, and heaven, and Milton's adventure highlights the consequences of the Fall of Adam and Eve.

To Do

Read Dante's *The Divine Comedy* and Milton's *Paradise Lost*. These two classics have illustrated the drama of salvation history in the popular mind like no other works.

To Journal

Copy down and reflect on these famous passages: "Keep clearly in mind the cause of your birth. You were not created as an unintelligent brute; go rather in pursuit of virtue and truth" (*The Divine Comedy*). "Is it not better to reign in hell than to serve in heaven?" (Satan in *Paradise Lost*)

Prayer

"Joy excelling, blissful dwelling/ Heaven, great city of the elect. Joy reigns there in song and laughter/ Happiness, beyond compare" ("*Paradiso*").

Try as you will, you cannot even begin to imagine the wonders I have prepared for you. But keep trying.

God's word

". . . [N]o eye has seen, nor ear heard, nor the heart of man conceived, what God has prepared for those who love him" (1 Corinthians 2:9).

Words of Wisdom

Imagination is so important. It stirs up hope and desire in us. Even if we haven't been blessed with a vivid imagination, we are probably all capable of imagining what we love, what delights us.

To do

Accustom yourself to thinking about death each night before falling asleep.

To journal

When the visionaries at Medjugorje began to describe what they had seen of heaven, people listening to them were disappointed. The fault lay not with heaven, but with the visionaries' inability to describe what they saw. Ivan, one of the visionaries, began to say simply, "You'll like it." What is an experience you have been unable to put into words?

Prayer

"O joyful gathering, O joyful gathering! Freely we'll speak with the blessed/ forever with Christ and Mary/ In the great company of all the saints" (*Paradiso*).

December 12

Let your charity extend beyond those living on earth.

God's Word

"I believe that I shall see the goodness of the LORD in the land of the living!" (Psalm 27:13) ". . . [I]f he was looking to the splendid reward that is laid up for those who fall asleep in godliness, it was a holy and pious thought" (2 Maccabees 12:45).

Words of Wisdom

In the Bible, the Maccabees offered sacrifices for the dead soldiers they found who had forbidden idols with them. This shows that God forgives sin even in the next life (cf. 2 Maccabees 12:46).

To Do

Pope Benedict XVI, in his encyclical *Sacrament of Charity*, encourages us to have Masses offered for the deceased. Have a Mass offered for a loved one or obtain for them a "perpetual Mass enrollment" (obtained through a religious congregation).

To Journal

Who are your loved ones that have gone before you? Who are famous people who have died that you feel drawn to pray for? Why?

Prayer

"His deep desire was for forgiveness/ He longed to see their liberty/ And His yearning was embodied/ In the Year of Jubilee" (Michael Card, "*Jubilee*").

December 13

The moment of death is a sacred moment. Surround the dying with much prayer.

God's Word

". . . [W]e have a building from God, a house not made with hands, eternal in the heavens" (2 Corinthians 5:1).

Words of Wisdom

Death is something we need to prepare for. It's the biggest trip we'll ever take!

To do

Learn about the Church's comforting "Commendation of the Dying," a ritual that can be used with the Sacrament of the Anointing of the Sick. (The sacrament, which used to be called the "Last Rites," is meant to either restore the person to health or bless them on their way to God.) The "Commendation" has stunningly beautiful prayers. Copy down some of these Scriptures or prayers. Pray them for the dying of the world.

To journal

If God gave you a choice, would you die suddenly or slowly? Why or why not?

Prayer

May you be led to paradise by angels; may martyrs accompany you to that holy city, Jerusalem, new and eternal. May choirs of angels welcome you directly to the arms of Abraham, where, with Lazarus who is no longer poor, you will find eternal rest (cf. Funeral Mass).

December 14

Why does the thought of your death make you sad? Don't you want to come to Me?

God's Word

"Lord Jesus, receive my spirit" (Acts 7:59).

Words of Wisdom

Every morning, thank God for all that has come before, tell Him you're ready whenever He wants to bring you home, and consciously set out to live the day as if it were your last. Bl. Pope John XXIII said, "I must get used to the thought of death, so that my life can thereby become more happy, vigorous, and energetic." The thought of our death should not make us morose. It will help us know what's important in life and to live it fully.

To Do

Use Susan Tassone's book *Prayers for Eternal Life*.

To journal

Bl. James Alberione said that if people consider themselves pragmatists and realists, they should be practical and realistic all the way through to eternity and get ready for it! How are you getting ready?

Prayer

Jesus, Mary, and Joseph, I give you my heart and my soul. Jesus, Mary, and Joseph, assist me in my last agony. Jesus, Mary, and Joseph, may I breathe forth my soul in peace with you.

December 15

There is no such thing as reincarnation. There is only one you—body and soul—that I have loved into being forever!

God's Word

". . . [I]t is appointed for men to die once, and after that comes judgment . . ." (Hebrews 9:27).

Words of Wisdom

There are many erroneous ideas about the afterlife in the popular culture gleaned from various religions. Many religions see time as cyclical: repeating itself over and over again without end. The Judeo-Christian understanding of time is linear. We are going somewhere to be with Someone! But in another sense, it *is* cyclical: we came from God and are going back to God!

To do

Research what criteria archaeologists use when trying to decide if ancient bones/remains are human or pre-human. (One thing they look for is preparations for the future and an afterlife.)

To journal

What are some of the confusing ideas about the afterlife that you've observed in popular culture?

Prayer

"We've come a mighty long way, Lord, a mighty long way. We've borne our burdens in the heat of the day. But we know the Lord has made the way. We've come a long way, Lord, a mighty long way" ("We've Come a Long Way").

December 16

When you die, you do not become angels in heaven, you remain human beings!

God's Word

"For my angel is with you, and he is watching over your lives" (Jeremiah 6:6 NRSV).

Words of Wisdom

Sometimes when a child dies, the family will say, "We have an angel in heaven." When someone does a kind deed we say, "You're an angel." What we really mean is that someone is *like* an angel.

To Do

Read the Book of Tobit in the Bible—a story of the Archangel Raphael taking on human form. What was his human name? Why is Raphael the patron of travel, eyes, and happy marriages?

To Journal

Have you given your guardian angel a name? If not, ask your angel to reveal his name to you. Journal about your reliance on your guardian angel. If you don't have a relationship with your guardian angel yet, write about how you plan to strike up an acquaintance.

Prayer

"I looked over the Jordan and what did I see, comin' for to carry me home? A band of angels comin' after me, comin' for to carry me home!" ("Swing Low, Sweet Chariot")

December 17

In heaven, there will be no more goodbyes, only hellos.

God's Word

"We know that we have passed out of death into life, because we love the brethren" (1 John 3:14).

Words of Wisdom

"Since I entered the monastery, my concept of death has changed radically. I'm not just speaking of physical death, but of that death to self that is so salutary. Now I don't know about you, but I tend to be a bit cowardly when it comes to denying myself. This is all the more reason why I (and you) must do it!" (Sr. John Mary of the Indwelling Trinity, CP, www.passionistnuns.org)

To do

Read Robert Frost's poem "Stopping by Woods on a Snowy Evening." What does he mean by "The woods are lovely, dark, and deep. But I have promises to keep, and miles to go before I sleep"?

To journal

What would you like people to remember about you when you're gone? Write your "last words," obituary, eulogy, or epitaph.

Prayer

Dear Lord, remember your promise to Abraham and his children and bring all the departed into the new life of heaven.

December 18

I do not send anyone to heaven or hell. Each person is free to go where they wish: to be with Me or without Me.

God's Word

"Into your hand I commit my spirit . . ." (Psalm 31:5 NRSV).

Words of Wisdom

Every day of our lives we are either choosing for God or against God. However, it doesn't stack up *quantitatively* because God is merciful. God can forgive all our sins in the twinkling of an eye. It does stack up *qualitatively,* though, because we will have trained our hearts to love or to not love God. Unfortunately, we've divorced heaven and hell from God. We've depersonalized it and made it all about a "place" that we go. But it's really about being with or away from God.

To Do

Read Sirach, chapter 5, in the Bible.

To Journal

Have you thought of heaven and hell in the terms mentioned above? If not, how does this view change your ideas about heaven and hell?

Prayer

"O Christ, do Thou my soul prepare for that bright home of love; that I may see Thee and adore with all Thy saints above" ("Jerusalem, My Happy Home").

December 19

Eternity is outside time. The laws of time do not apply to eternity. Time is a created thing that had its beginning with creation.

God's Word

"Like a drop of water from the sea and a grain of sand so are a few years in the day of eternity" (Sirach 18:10).

Words of Wisdom

Eternal means no beginning and no end. Only God is eternal. When we die, we join God in His eternity, which is outside of time. There are some things we will never be able to wrap our minds around.

To do

Read Psalm 90 prayerfully. Write out your favorite lines.

To journal

Write out this description of eternity: Once every billion years, a little bird brushes its wing against the tip of a mountain. The time it takes to wear down the mountain is one nano-second of eternity.

Prayer

"My name is called and I must go, and I heard from heaven today. Hurry on, my weary soul, and I heard from heaven today" ("I Heard From Heaven Today").

December 20

You are very great. How can you know that to be true? I became one of you, and I am still one of you.

God's Word

"In his hand is the life of every living thing and the breath of all mankind" (Job 12:10).

Words of Wisdom

Cremation used to be forbidden for Catholics because it was seen as not honoring the body. It is now allowed as long as one has a firm belief in the resurrection of the body and inters the ashes.

To Do

Learn about the burial customs of various cultures and religions. For example, for some, the greatest way to honor the body is to give it to the vultures so it will rejoin the circle of life. How prevalent do you think embalming is?

To Journal

What do you think of Gunther von Hagens's "Body Worlds" exhibitions?

Prayer

"I'll take Jesus for my Savior, you take Him too, look away beyond the blue horizon. Do, Lord, O do, Lord, O do remember me" ("Do, Lord, Remember Me").

December 21

Even though you have faith in Me, the pain of losing a loved one to death is still immense.

"Jesus wept" (John 11:35).

Asian and African cultures have great respect for their ancestors. However, the deceased need not have an oppressive, controlling presence in our lives. They have gone to God, and we have to live our own lives. First and foremost, we are God's. We all belong to God.

Read the poem "Safely Home," or the book *Praying Our Goodbyes* by Joyce Rupp. Create an online photo album or a scrapbook, or decorate a wall in your house to remember deceased relatives and friends. Learn more about your ancestors, biological or adopted. Ask people who still remember them to tell you facts and stories about their lives. Write them down for future generations.

There is no timetable for grief when you lose someone. Whom have you lost already? What has your grief process been like?

"We are traveling in the footsteps of those who've gone before, and we'll all be reunited on a new and sunlit shore" ("When the Saints Go Marching In").

December 22

I love you and your loved ones more than you do! I want you all in heaven with Me more than you do!

God's word

"Father, I desire that those also, whom you have given me, may be with me where I am . . ." (John 17:24 NRSV).

Words of wisdom

We pray for the dead and ask them to pray for us, but we may never try to contact them through channeling, spirit guides, mediums, or séances (cf. *Catechism of the Catholic Church*, nos. 2110–2117). Evil spirits often take advantage of our imprudent openness and impersonate the dead.

To do

Sometimes the Lord permits a deceased person to appear in order for the living to pray for them, or to console the living. We should accept these things with peace when they happen, but always discern the spirits. If you're uncertain, consult a wise priest.

To journal

If the Lord let you come back just once after your death, who would you appear to? What would you do or say?

Prayer

"Sit at my Jesus's feet, Jesus's feet, Sit at my Jesus's feet, O Mary, O Martha, sit at my Jesus's feet" ("Wish I Was in Heaven Settin' Down").

December 23

I have revealed the end to you. It is a good end because I am good, and because I created you good, for goodness.

God's word

"Where, O death, is your sting?" (1 Corinthians 15:55 NRSV) "Come, O blessed of my Father, inherit the kingdom prepared for you from the foundation of the world" (Matthew 25:34).

Words of wisdom

We are all terminal! If today you were to die, what would you want to have changed about your life? What would you want to have done differently? What would you wish you had done? Well, this probably *isn't* the last day of your life, so what are you waiting for?

To do

Read John Donne's poem "Death Be Not Proud." Watch *Wit* starring Emma Thompson which is considered the greatest film ever made about a terminally-ill patient.

To journal

Do you find life is more like a test, a journey, an ordeal, an adventure, a mystery, a puzzle, a story, a dance, or something else? Describe what you find life to be.

Prayer

May Your everlasting light shine on those who have died, Lord. In Your mercy let them rejoice with Your saints for all eternity.

December 24

You cannot put a limit to My mercy. It is endless.

God's word

"And when I go and prepare a place for you, I will come again and will take you to myself, that where I am you may be also" (John 14:3).

Words of wisdom

Even those whose lives seem to end tragically or who seem to have wasted their lives, have a last chance at the moment of death— a secret meeting between themselves and God, unobservable to outsiders. Every life can have a happy "Hollywood" ending.

To do

Pray the Divine Mercy chaplet for the most desperate souls. Always include the "Fatima Prayer" after the "Glory Be" when you say the Rosary.

To journal

Without God's mercy, no one would be saved. We are all in need of God's mercy. Even if we're not "big sinners," remember: "To whom more is given, more will be expected." For what do you feel you need God's mercy most?

Prayer

"If you get there before I do, comin' for to carry me home! Tell all my friends I'm comin' after you, comin' for to carry me home!" ("Swing Low, Sweet Chariot").

December 25

I was born in a borrowed stable and was laid in a borrowed tomb. Will you still follow me?

God's word

"The last enemy to be destroyed is death" (1 Corinthians 15:26).

Words of wisdom

Jesus was born to die. The Magi brought the burial gift of myrrh. Herod wanted to kill baby Jesus. His Mother was prophesied to be Our Lady of Sorrows. After celebrating the feast of Christmas, we celebrate the Holy Innocents and other martyrs. Birth is linked with death. Our death date can be seen as our birthday into heaven.

To do

If Jesus has conquered death, why do we still die? It is because "death is the last enemy to be destroyed." For now, we must still go through death as He did. However, heaven is opened. Jesus is waiting on the other side.

To journal

Jesus is a true Messiah. Jesus drives out our fears. Jesus harrows hell. What "bullies" surrounding death do you want Jesus to take care of for you?

Prayer

"Jubilee, Jubilee/ Jesus is our Jubilee/ Debts forgiven/ Slaves set free/ Jesus is our Jubilee" (Michael Card, *Jubilee*).

December 26

Some experience life as more sad than happy. Be merciful to others, be merciful to yourself.

God's Word

"The years of our life are . . . but toil and trouble; they are soon gone, and we fly away" (Psalm 90:10).

Words of Wisdom

A big part of the Divine Mercy devotion is extending mercy to others in imitation of God. Mercy is not simply an act of forgiveness, but having the same attitude that God has toward our fellow human beings. Pray to have a merciful heart. "Love your enemies and pray for those who persecute you" (Matthew 5:44).

To do

Listen to The Byrd's famous song from the '60s: "Turn! Turn! Turn!" (cf. Ecclesiastes 3:1–8). Read *Surviving Depression* or *Prayers for Surviving Depression* (both by Sr. Kathryn Hermes, FSP) for yourself or others.

To journal

Copy this thought of Corrie ten Boom, Dutch Christian Holocaust survivor and rescuer of Jews: "There is no pit so deep that God is not deeper still." To whom do I most need to show mercy?

Prayer

"I'm sometimes up, I'm sometimes down, comin' for to carry me home! But still my soul feels heaven bound, comin' for to carry me home!" ("Swing Low, Sweet Chariot").

December 27

There is nothing new under the sun except the new life I offer you!

God's word

"Remember also your Creator in the days of your youth, before the evil days come . . . when you will say, 'I have no pleasure in them'" (Ecclesiastes 12:1). "Vanity of vanities . . . all is vanity" (Ecclesiastes 12:8).

Words of wisdom

Sometimes life just is what it is. Read Marcus Aurelius's (yes, the Emperor who killed Christians) *Meditations*. He had a realistic acceptance of life (but without Christian hope).

To do

Read the Book of Ecclesiastes in the Bible. Does it bring you down? Does it give you hope? Does it make you laugh?

To journal

When did you first become aware of death? Whose was the first wake or funeral you attended? How was death first explained to you? How has the thought of your own mortality affected you throughout your life?

Prayer

"I've got a song, you've got a song, all of God's children got a song. When I get to heaven, gonna sing a new song, gonna sing all over God's heaven!" ("Gonna Shout All Over God's Heaven").

December 28

Forever is a long time.

God's word

"For what does it profit a man if he gains the whole world and loses or forfeits himself?" (Luke 9:25)

Words of wisdom

Everyone reads Milton's *Paradise Lost*, but they forget to read his *Paradise Regained*. Don't forget, as Bl. Pope John XXIII said, "We move toward heaven from every different point of earth, yet the path to get there always follows the cross."

To do

Research the meaning of "saint" as used in Scripture (meaning "Christians"), and what a "canonized" saint is.

To journal

Does saint mean a goody-goody to you? Many saints didn't start off very goody-goody. The saints were red-blooded, passionate, diverse, and fascinating individuals. Saint simply means holy, and holy means best friends with God. The saints were all good at one thing: love. How good are you at loving?

Prayer

"I'll go to see her [Mary] one day: this is the cry that gives me hope, and strengthens me in constancy in this journey passing through trials. I'll go to see her one day, leaving behind me this exile. And as a child who's home at last, I'll place my head on her heart" ("*Andro a Vederla*").

December 29

Do not go running here and there when people say, "It's the Messiah!" You will know. Everyone will know.

God's Word

"For as the lightning flashes and lights up the sky . . . so will the Son of man be in his day" (Luke 17:24).

Words of Wisdom

There are many wrong and harmful ideas about Jesus's Second Coming: the so-called rapture; the idea that *we* have to make Jesus come again by creating war in the Middle East; the idea that when Jesus comes, it won't be the end of the world and some will be left behind. All these ideas come from misreading Scripture. Read the *Catechism of the Catholic Church* (nos. 1038–1041), and *The Rapture Trap* by Paul Thigpen, to understand the Second Coming.

To Do

Pray the alternate (Vatican-approved) Glorious Mysteries of the Rosary: the Fourth Glorious Mystery is the Assumption *and* Coronation of Mary, and the Fifth Glorious Mystery is the Second Coming of Jesus.

To Journal

When Jesus comes, would you prefer to be living or already dead? Why?

Prayer

"I'll go to see her one day, in paradise, my fatherland. I'll see my Mother Mary, my joy and my love" ("*Andro a Vederla*").

December 30

Is your love for the earth why you don't want to leave it? Why you don't want to die? Fear not. I make all things new.

"... I create new heavens and a new earth; and the former things shall not be remembered or come into mind" (Isaiah 65:17).

We should never worry that we will miss something in heaven that we loved here on earth. Will there be dogs in heaven? Of course.

After the Fall, God made a new and better plan that includes the renewal of this beautiful earth. Why would God just get rid of all this stuff that He made and loves? Recite the lyrics of Pierpont's hymn "For the Beauty of the Earth." Read the *Catechism of the Catholic Church* (nos. 1042–1050).

When you listen to the sounds of nature: crickets, birdsong, the wind in the trees, a babbling brook, and rain, what do they seem to be saying?

"Some say this world of trouble is the only one we need, but I'm waiting for that morning when the new world is revealed" ("When the Saints Go Marching In").

December 31

What will separate you from My love? Nothing. If I am for you, who can be against you? No one.

God's Word

"We love, because he first loved us" (1 John 4:19).

Words of Wisdom

The final stage of our transformation in Christ is often called Christification. Focus on, aim for, pray for, and desire your transformation in Christ.

To do

Remember that everything is all about *Him*. We are God's children because *Jesus* is God's first-born. We get to be part of something much bigger than ourselves. We get to be part of God's life. We have been given an exclusive backstage pass because of *Him*. We have been raised up to an entirely new dignity and glory because of *Him*. It's all about *Him*. Let us never stop thanking and praising *Him* for *He is worthy*!

To journal

Write *Him* a prayer of praise.

Prayer

"Now to him who by the power at work within us is able to do far more abundantly than all that we ask or think, to him be glory in the church and in Christ Jesus to all generations, for ever and ever. Amen" (Ephesians 3:20–21).

Acknowledgments

Lyrics from the song "Jubilee" by Michael Card © 1989 Birdwing Music (ASCAP) (adm. At EMICMGPublishing.com). All rights reserved. Used by permission.

Lyrics from the song "House of Peace" by Jim Croegaert © 1974, 1991, Rough Stones Music Co. (ASCAP), Evanston, IL. All rights reserved. Used by permission.

Lyrics from the song "Love Is a Commitment" by Larry Norman © 1991, Solid Rock Productions, Inc., Salem, OR. All rights reserved. Used by permission.

The permission to reproduce copyrighted materials from *What Does God Want? A Practical Guide to Making Decisions* by Michael Scanlan, was extended by Our Sunday Visitor, 200 Noll Plaza, Huntington, IN 46750. 1-800-348-2440. Website: www.osv.com. No other use of this material is authorized.

Excerpt from an untitled speech by Christopher West is used with permission granted by Ascension Press, West Chester, PA.

Sources

www.paulinemedia.com

www.greatadventureonline.com

www.saintjoe.com

www.salvationhistory.com

ssvmusa.org/

www.ascensionpress.com

www.vatican.va

www.Biblegateway.com

BOOKS & MEDIA

A mission of the Daughters of St. Paul

As apostles of Jesus Christ, evangelizing today's world:

We are CALLED to holiness
by God's living Word and Eucharist.

We COMMUNICATE the Gospel message
through our lives and through all
available forms of media.

We SERVE the Church
by responding to the hopes and needs
of all people with the Word of God,
in the spirit of St. Paul.

For more information visit our website: www.pauline.org.

BOOKS & MEDIA

The Daughters of St. Paul operate book and media centers at the following addresses. Visit, call or write the one nearest you today, or find us on the World Wide Web, www.pauline.org

¡También somos su fuente para libros,
videos y música en español!